THE ADVENTURER'S GUIDE
TO THE OUTDOORS

THE ADVENTURER'S GUIDE
TO THE OUTDOORS

100 Essential Skills for Surviving in the Wild

UNIVERSE

First published in 2013 by Universe Publishing
A Division of Rizzoli International Publications, Inc.
300 Park Avenue South
New York, NY 10010
www.rizzoliusa.com

See full publisher's disclaimer p. 9

General Editor: Sarah Perrem
Illustration and Design: Sam Chelton
Project Editor: Henry Dieterich
Project Editor: Candice Fehrman
Production: Michelle Woo

2013 2014 2015 2016 / 10 9 8 7 6 5 4 3 2 1

ISBN-13: 978-0-7893-2477-1

Library of Congress Catalog Control Number: 2012955014; British Library Cataloguing-in-Publication Data: a catalogue record for this book is available from the British Library.

Printed in China

CONTENTS

FOREWORD

"Why did you want to climb Mount Everest?"
"Because it's there."
— *George Mallory's famous retort before his final attempt on Mount Everest in 1924*

The Adventurer's Guide to the Outdoors assumes the reader is neither qualified nor unqualified for any of the guidance that the book provides. With regard to the editorial selection, the reader is assumed to be in different scenarios (such as in need of finding water or a suitable campsite), and is given ideas at a basic or beginner's level about how to go about the task. The variety of skills, insights, and advice are intended for all readers. With regard to terrain, equipment, and capability, the book assumes that the reader is in command of his senses, able-bodied, and has access to some basic equipment, such as a knife—however, some chapters discuss techniques that assume there are no tools to hand. The chapters are accompanied by diagrams and descriptions that are hopefully easy to understand and practically useable by anyone. Again, each chapter is by no means an exhaustive study, nor is any scenario pursued to its full extent; this is not a Bible for the explorer, but a snapshot of some of the many techniques and skills that the reader can learn.

PUBLISHER'S DISCLAIMER

The Adventurer's Guide to the Outdoors is a collection of skills and advice that has been compiled by experts in outdoorsmanship. This book should not be used as a *survival* guide in the purest sense; it is by no means an exhaustive guide to survival, regardless of the climate or terrain, although the contents are entirely reliable and could be useful in life outdoors in the wilderness. When planning an expedition of any scale that requires careful study and preparation, use this book only as a companion of the entertaining, if informative, sort. The publisher can accept no responsibility for any injury caused in the practice of these techniques, nor for any prosecution relating to the treatment of land or animals that may adhere directly or indirectly to the techniques described in this book. The reader should assume full responsibility for any practical use of any of the actions described, and make full inquiries into the legality of using them before doing so.

INTRODUCTION BY GUY GRIEVE

I am a great believer in the importance of spending time in the outdoors, and learning how to do it well. In today's world, it is easy to become disconnected from the joy and profound fulfillment that come from learning how to live successfully in a wild place. It is vital to remember that we are part of something so much more important and bigger than us, something that is not necessarily predictable or controllable. Stepping into a wilderness zone, although initially daunting, can be a very positive life-defining experience. On the other hand, it can be a mournful and unhappy experience if we do not take care to step carefully and with humility.

Twice in my life I have been lucky enough to spend long periods totally immersed in the wilderness. First, I traveled into the interior of Alaska, where I built a cabin and lived alone for one year, 300 miles from the nearest paved road. I was lucky enough to meet an old woodsman, who taught me the fundamentals of how to live safely and comfortably even in one of the world's seemingly most inhospitable environments. I hunted grouse and beaver, dug snow holes, and traveled by dog team. The Yukon River became my highway, by boat in the summer and by dog sled in the frozen depths of winter. If you work with nature instead of trying to beat it, I discovered, you can live very well.

Some years later, and this time not alone but with my wife and children, I went to live at sea. An old sailing boat became our planet and the sea our universe as we journeyed thousands of miles from South America back to our home on an island off the west coast of Scotland. During those windswept watery days, the flukes of our anchor dug deeply into safe harbor beside many remote islands and strips of coastline. Again, I found myself utterly immersed in nature, and the joy was much increased by sharing the experience with my family.

Although completely different, these two environments had something in common. In both, I was lucky enough to meet people who did not tread all over nature, but instead lived simply and well within it. The landscape sustained them, as they grew vegetables and hunted in the woods and seas around them. They knew how to work with nature, to draw the best from it without leaning on it too hard. In return, the outdoors sustained them both physically and psychologically, and I saw a contentment that is rarely seen in our comfortable world.

I loved those days during which the sea became our home, but even more I enjoyed seeing how our two boys thrived and grew from the experience of being totally immersed in nature. They learned the vagaries of weather and the sea, and the importance of working with nature and not against it. They learned to be self-sufficient and careful, to entertain themselves without gadgets or technology, and to live slowly and quietly in tune with nature's rhythms. They learned to stay calm and think clearly in the face of danger; to respect yet not fear wild animals. Being outdoors all the time, they grew physically confident and strong, ate healthily, and slept well. Most vitally, they learned that, whatever our environment, we need very little to sustain us—just food, basic shelter, and a little company.

It is in this "boyish" spirit that I want you to read this book. Not to set out to conquer nature or pit your wits against it in the spirit of many of the "adventure" outdoor TV series that are all too common, but rather to step lightly and learn to enjoy what is around you. This book is not a guide designed to turn you into a Navy Seal or backwoods survivalist. It is just a little prompt, a few pointers that might help you start exploring the idea of existing outdoors simply and well. Take the advice, but don't get too lost in it all. Common sense and patience and humility are by far the most important components to moving around in wild places.

We don't need much to be happy—a stand of trees, a beach, a river or stream. It takes a little time to become truly adept at being comfortable outdoors, but the more we practice speaking nature's language, the more fluent we become. Don't charge around—do things slowly and take time to drink it all in. Listen to the wind in the treetops, watch the patterns of water rippling over river rocks, inhale the subtle scent of new growth in the spring. Cook on a small fire made of light twigs, witness the sun rising and setting, and gaze up at the stars. With just a little quiet learning and plenty of trial and error, being in the outdoors can be a comfortable and rewarding experience.

In the course of your learning, get ready to take a few bumps and knocks along the way. Nothing truly real comes without a little pain—relish it, as it makes your hard-earned comfort all the more worthwhile. If you can find your way within nature's wilder regions, you will be learning so much more than the basics of lighting fires and various other skills. You will be finding a place that will always be there for you, feeding and sustaining you in times of joy and trouble. Hopefully, in doing so, you will discover how precious it is, and will enter the fight to defend our wild places against people who think all we need in order to eat is money.

BOOK ONE

GETTING READY

1
PLAN YOUR JOURNEY, GEAR, AND SUPPLIES

THE LIST

All great adventures should start with a humble list. You need to decide where you are going, and how long your adventure will last, and proceed to write your list.

LIST OF THINGS TO BUY

- Local maps and a compass
- Suitable tent, backpack, and sleeping bag
- First aid kit
- Survival guide
- Travel guide to the area
- Knife
- GPS
- Fishing line and hooks

LIST OF THINGS TO DO

- Pick a person to notify of your travel plans (best is someone who will notice if you do not return).
- Learn how to light a fire without matches.
- Practice putting up your tent in the backyard.
- Get a scout who's passing by to teach you how to use a map and compass.
- Tie some knots.
- Sharpen your knife.
- Find your old fishing gear and hooks.
- Learn first aid.

RESEARCH

Will there be alligators? Do you need to pack bear pepper spray? How hot will it be? What are the signs of hypothermia and what *is* hypothermia? What do you do if there is a forest fire?

Use the Internet, go to the library, or browse your local bookshop to find out all about your destination, climate, and potential hazards. Find out as much as you can about the area. If you are planning on foraging in the wild, make sure you know how to distinguish between safe and poisonous plants and bring a few photocopies of detailed pictures to help you.

WEATHER

Many an adventure has been spoiled by rain or an unexpected hurricane. Long-range weather forecasts should be checked well in advance of your trip. Heavy snow will necessitate different equipment than a trip during the tropical rainy season.

FIND A FRIEND

It is always safer to travel in a group. It also enables you to share the carrying of heavy items, and possibly to allocate camp duties, such as digging the latrine. If possible, find an easygoing, fit friend who is well versed in survival techniques and first aid, and likes putting up tents. It is even better if they already own all the expensive gear you will need.

GO TO THE BANK

Sadly, while the great outdoors does not usually have an entrance fee, all the gear and supplies you will be carrying around and wearing can cost a great deal. Careful planning should eliminate unnecessary purchases, as will borrowing from kindly neighbors and friends. There are plenty of low-cost alternatives if you give yourself time to research. You may determine that it is cheaper to purchase what you need at your destination.

2
KNOW YOUR CLIMATE, TERRAIN, AND WEATHER

There are many types of climates in the world. Understanding the climate in which you will be traveling, and the terrain you will experience, will help you plan a safe, enjoyable trip.

CLIMATE TYPES

The main climate types to be aware of are the following:

- Temperate grasslands and forests of America and Eurasia
- Mediterranean
- Northern coniferous forests
- Polar regions
- Deserts
- Tropical regions

Each climate has challenges for the traveler. The easiest climates and terrains to travel in are the temperate, forested areas of America and Eurasia. There is plenty of food to hunt and forage, plenty of water, the weather does not present survival challenges unless you travel at high altitude, and there is an abundance of materials for fires and shelter.

The Mediterranean climate and region is sparser in available wildlife and has harsher, drier summers. It would be more difficult to locate food and water year-round.

Colder regions like the northern coniferous forests of Europe and Asia present other difficulties. There is plenty of food to hunt, but less to forage. You are more likely to suffer cold, damp, or snowy conditions.

The polar regions have difficult terrain, and the weather requires specialist gear. It is possible to hunt and fish in these regions, but finding material to build shelters with is difficult. Weather updates are essential to avoid getting stranded in heavy snow.

Deserts vary greatly in type depending on the area of the world. They may be sandy, rocky and barren, or mountainous. What they have in common is their wide range of temperature from day to night, low rainfall, intense sunlight, and sparse vegetation. The climate makes finding water and surviving the heat your primary concerns. Sandstorms or dust storms occur almost once a week in nearly all deserts of the world, and winds can reach up to 80 mph (130 kph).

Nearly every type of life thrives in tropical regions, and this includes bacteria. The weather there will be humid, hot, and wet. Flooding is common, as are monsoons, hurricanes, and tidal waves, depending on your exact location and the season. Violent storms are more common toward the end of the summer. Day and night are of equal length in the tropics. Food and materials can be found in abundance, but the heat makes the storage of food almost impossible.

3
CHOOSE SUITABLE CLOTHING

There is no such thing as bad weather, only unsuitable clothing. Wear the correct clothes for the climate and weather, and make sure they fit you. You will then look the part, feel comfortable, and avoid unnecessary chafing as you travel. Good outdoor adventure shops and army surplus stores are good places to start looking.

THE BEST FABRICS

If you are traveling in the tropics or in a warm, summer climate, light cotton is the best choice. Light linen will also keep you cool, but you will be sporting a more crushed, slept-in look. If you are in a more moderate climate and altitude, you can be more flexible. Cotton, wool, and many synthetic fibers will work. Fleece is a lightweight, easily dried material that can provide a quick extra layer.

If you are traveling in the winter, at higher altitudes, or in colder regions, wool is your best friend. Layering thin wool tops will keep you very warm while allowing your skin to breathe. Unlike many synthetic materials, it will even keep you insulated when wet. This is why none of the sheep in Ireland have permanent colds and flu. There is expensive specialty gear, which, if you are traveling in polar regions, you should consider. You will only be limited by how much money you wish to spend. It is possible to purchase lightweight jackets that are lined with goose down, which will keep you very warm.

LAYER UP

Except in very hot tropical regions, it is best to wear multiple layers and to take spare clothes with you, especially clean socks. Air is trapped between the layers and will insulate you against cold. Layering will also allow you greater control of how warmly you wish to dress at various times during the day.

WHAT NOT TO WEAR

Do not wear denim. Denim absorbs water and does not dry quickly. It sticks to your skin and causes your body temperature to

fall rapidly. Other things to avoid, in all climates, are flip-flops, sandals, or other soft shoes. Not only do you risk being bitten by insects, spiders, and snakes, but you also increase your chances of picking up leeches and ticks, and getting cuts and scrapes. All injuries and bites can result in infection, so avoidance is best.

Avoid shorts and short-sleeved tops. Even rain-soaked clothes will protect your skin from sunburn, bites, and scratches.

WATERPROOFS

In nearly all climates, except the desert, a waterproof poncho or jacket long enough to sit on should be packed. This will protect you from windchill and unexpected showers. It can be used as a groundsheet or even as a makeshift tent if you get caught outdoors overnight. Even in warm climates you should avoid getting wet if possible.

HEADGEAR

Don't forget your hat. Remember to consider your needs when shopping and then let your own style lead you. Are you ready to try out a balaclava, or does the brightly colored bobble hat take your fancy? In the tropics, a sun hat will work better. When hiking in the summer, a hat with a brim is best, as it will protect you from sunburn. Many hikers recommend packing a wool hat, even in summer, as overnight it can be used to keep you warm and to cushion your head like a pillow.

SHOES

Take note: sandals have already been ruled out. For all outdoor adventures, you will need a pair of good, well-fitting hiking boots. Spend as much money as you can afford on your shoes and get advice from one or two specialty shops before you buy. Your choice of boots will vary hugely depending on the terrain and climate and what your needs are. Will you be walking in flat, humid country or up steep inclines at high altitude? You should wear thick socks with the boots that you buy for your trip. Before your adventure, you should wear new boots often to break them in. Suitable footwear will enable you to walk farther and with less risk of injury, strain, or blisters. The boots should have thick enough soles to protect your feet, and if you are hiking over rough terrain, they should provide ankle support, too. Before you buy shoes, ask the following:

• How waterproof are they?
• How robust are they?
• Are they cushioned for long hikes?
• Do they have adequate grips on the sole?
• How expensive are they?

4
PACK WISELY

Packing wisely will save you backaches and heartaches and unnecessary headaches.

WEIGHT

The average fit person can hike for a day carrying 25–30 pounds (11–14 kilograms). This should be the maximum you plan to carry. Packing light will require planning carefully and sourcing as much lightweight equipment as possible. Avoid tin cans and bring light packets of dry soup instead. Buy lightweight camping stoves and sleeping bags. Know what is essential and what constitutes a luxury item. Use your bathroom scale and remove extra items or share them among others in the group if your pack is too heavy.

PACKING

When packing, consider placing all items in plastic bags and lining your backpack with a foam mat, if you have one, or your bivvy (waterproof survival bag). Even the best waterproof backpack can let moisture in, especially if you have to hike for several hours in the pouring rain. Cushion yourself against hard or sharp items by wrapping them in clothing. Ensure that items such as rations for your day and your map and compass are easily accessible, in zipped side pockets. Pack heavy items at the top of your bag, but make sure the bag is not too top-heavy. Test your bag to make sure that it is well balanced, that the weight rests evenly on each shoulder. Uneven packing may lead to bad posture, chafing, or sideways falls.

YOUR BAG

Bags come in many shapes, styles, colors, and capacities. If you are planning a long trip or foresee a series of outdoor adventures in your future, you should invest in a good bag. It should be waterproof, lined, and have some side pockets with zippers and some internal pockets. Most backpacks these days are designed with internal frames so you can make your way more easily through brush and along rocky crags without getting snagged on something as you pass by. The good packs have some mesh between the pack and your back to allow a flow of air. Make sure the bag itself is not too heavy or you will meet your weight limit without much in the bag. Avoid bags that are much wider than the width of your body, or you may find yourself stuck in undergrowth or unable to hike gamely along a cliff face.

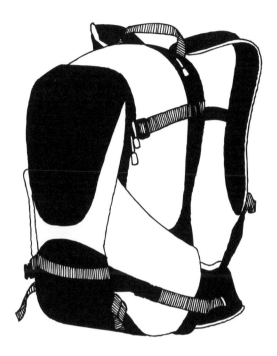

HOW MUCH TO PACK

How much to pack will depend on the length and type of your journey. If you are traveling in a group, you will probably be sharing items, such as a larger first aid kit or a tent or rations. You should always make allowances for the unexpected and include extra rations in case your journey takes longer than planned. The following is a quick guide to what to pack for your own personal use for a variety of hiking trips when you will be carrying your gear in relatively temperate climates.

For a one-day hike in pleasant conditions, include a first aid kit, compass and map, waterproofs, two two-liter bottles of water, emergency rations, matches, magnifying glass, daily rations, bivvy bag, watch, spare socks, and toilet paper.

For a one-day hike on higher ground, include everything listed above and also pack some warm clothes, rope, and a flashlight with spare batteries. In cold weather include everything above plus a flask of a hot drink, hat, sleeping bag, and extra clothes.

IF PLANNING TO CAMP

If you are planning to camp overnight, include everything above and also pack a tent, lightweight stove, food rations, fish hook and line, needle and thread, lightweight foam mat (to insulate you from damp ground), complete change of clothes, larger first aid bag, water bag, and sterilization tablets. A signal flare, cell phone or radio, and GPS may also be packed. In places where bears, raccoons, or other scavengers may be your nighttime neighbors, pack a long rope and a mesh bag so you can hang all your food from a high tree limb, far from their clever claws.

WHAT TO PACK FOR FIRST AID

If you are traveling far from home, you may wish to consider purchasing a region-specific first aid pack. Your first aid kit should, at minimum, contain the following:

- Pain reliever
- Diarrhea treatment
- Antihistamine
- Water sterilization tablets
- Hand sanitizer
- Band-Aids
- Bandages
- Two surgical blades of varying sizes
- Butterfly sutures
- One full course of a general antibiotic

WHAT ARE EMERGENCY RATIONS?

Apart from your daily or camp rations, you should each carry a supply of emergency rations. These should be lightweight, high-energy foods that can be used if a member of your party starts showing signs of hypothermia, or if an accident or bad weather unexpectedly lengthens your journey. Include glucose sweets, high-energy bars, dried fruit and nuts, extra water purification tablets, and packets of dried soup. Each person should carry their own emergency rations and some first aid equipment in case your party gets separated. If you are partial to nuts as you hike, include these in your normal daily rations. Munching on emergency rations is unacceptable.

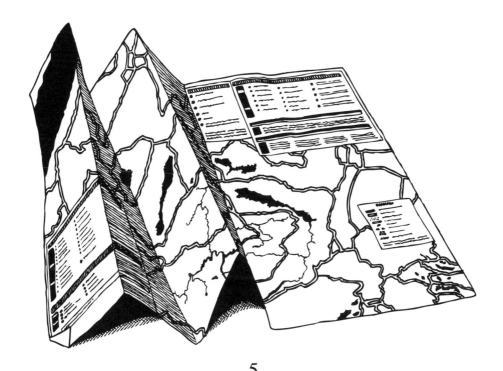

5

PLAN YOUR ROUTE AND THE SUPPLIES YOU'LL NEED

Planning the route means knowing how long and over what type of terrain you will be traveling. It will then be possible to pack adequate supplies.

WHY PLAN?

How far can you walk in a day with a full pack on your back? This is a question that you need to answer. If you are planning on traveling to a particular campsite, you need to know if you can reasonably achieve this in a one-day hike. Overestimating your fitness or underestimating the harshness of the terrain could lead to an uncomfortable night spent on a mountain.

TAKE OUT YOUR MAP

Before leaving the safety of your house, sit down with your map. Even a daily hike in a local area should be planned. Pay special attention to any contour lines that would indicate steep slopes or obstructions like rivers. Now, plot your route in short two-mile (three-kilometer) stages, or shorter, depending on when the terrain changes. Using the scale of the map and a ruler, estimate the distance you will actually travel.

ESTIMATED TIME OF ARRIVAL

It will now be necessary to do some small calculations. You can expect to conservatively travel around one mile (one and a half kilometers) in 20 minutes. If the terrain is rough, you should allow only two and a half miles (four kilometers) per hour. Steep inclines will add more time. For every 500 feet (150 meters) you ascend, you must add another 20 minutes to your previously calculated travel time. You must also add in time to rest. For every hour you travel, you should allow 15 minutes of rest. This does not mean you have to stop every hour, but five hours of hiking will actually take six hours and 15 minutes including rest times.

WALKING SLOWER
TAKES LONGER

Are you traveling over particularly difficult terrain or carrying extra gear? Are you traveling in hot or humid conditions? You will need to increase the frequency of your rest periods and decrease the number of hours you plan to walk in the whole day. In difficult terrain, rest periods of 15 minutes should be added every 40 minutes, and you can expect your speed to decrease toward the end of the day, so for a daily average, allow 30 minutes per mile (one and a half kilometers). This means that a 12-mile (20-kilometer) hike on a humid day may take you more than eight hours including rest.

If you are traveling through snow, reduce your calculations in a similar way. If the snow is deep or you are traveling through high winds, a blizzard, or torrential rain, you may only travel half the distance in the time you had originally allotted.

SUPPLIES

The route and time you take will help determine what gear you should bring. If you need to reach a certain point and it will take more than a reasonable day's hike, you will need to pack a tent, for example. You should always consider packing gear in case of emergencies. Mist may drive you down a mountain and lengthen your journey. You may need extra food or gear to enable you to spend a night outdoors. More details are given in the guide to packing.

DAILY RATIONS

Planning the route will enable you to correctly plan the gear you need. You will also need to correctly estimate rations of food. Not eating can lead to irritation, dizziness, nausea, and a lack of motivation to continue hiking.

At minimum, each person will need 2,200 calories per day. Vigorous exercise and fresh air will probably increase this to 3,000. You can increase your rations with healthy nuts, seeds and dried fruit, and not-so-healthy chocolate. It is possible to purchase freeze-dried daily rations for hiking. Be aware that many of these rations require soaking and cooking and are not suitable for eating on the go.

Items to seriously consider, which need no fire to prepare, include:

- Tuna and crackers with a small restaurant mayonnaise pack for flavor
- Hard cheese and crackers or bagels
- Peanut butter (removed from heavy jar)
- Candy
- Dried fruit

6
TRAVEL SAFELY

There will be region-specific safety issues to consider when you travel. For instance, you should never travel in a desert without bringing water. Also, when driving long distances through a sparsely populated area, you should always carry a spare tire. It is also good advice to never approach a large alligator and offer it food.

SOME GENERAL TIPS

Some advice is very specific, but there are also some general tips for safe travel that will apply regardless of where you travel.

PACK FOR SAFETY

- Carry emergency food.
- Carry water sterilization tablets.
- Carry spare clothes.
- Carry matches and flint.
- Carry a first aid kit.
- Bring a compass and map.

PLAN FOR SAFETY

- Always travel in a group.
- Plan your route and pack supplies accordingly.
- Estimate travel times based on the least fit member of your party.
- Learn first aid.

- Bring a radio, GPS, or cell phone.
- Know how to use your compass and map.
- Know how to light a fire.

SAFETY IN AN EMERGENCY

- Carry a flare and know how to use it.
- Ensure you have notified others of your planned route and estimated time of your trip.
- Make a contingency plan in case of illness, accident, or sudden severe weather.
- Have a rendezvous point planned in case you become separated.
- Ensure everyone has emergency food, matches, and first aid in their own bag.

RESEARCH FOR SAFETY

- Keep in touch with updated weather forecasts for your area.
- Know what dangerous predators live in the area and how to evade them.
- Know what poisonous snakes, insects, fish, or plants are in the area.
- Know what food in the area can be safely foraged and eaten.
- Know what alternative routes to take should an emergency necessitate a quick return to civilization.

DRESS FOR SAFETY

- Wear appropriate clothing to ensure you remain warm and dry.
- Wear appropriate footwear.
- Do not forget to apply sunscreen.
- Apply correct insect repellent for the area to avoid insects, mosquitoes, leeches, and ticks.

7
CHOOSE A KNIFE AND HOW TO SHARPEN IT

HOW TO CHOOSE
A KNIFE FOR YOUR JOURNEY

If you are only going to carry one knife, consider something stronger than a multi-bladed pocketknife. A blade for multiple purposes, with a wooden handle, is ideal, with the knife tang passing through the handle and fastened at the far end; the chances of getting blisters with this kind of handle are minimal. If the journey will require cutting through growth, chopping wood, and finer cutting, then a Malaysian *parang* is possibly ideal.

The tip of the *parang* and the section nearest the tip are fine and can be used for skinning animals and similar work, while the middle can be used for hacking and chopping wood. Nearer the handle the blade is more delicate and can be used for carving and exact work. A sheath will be needed. Ensure it is of good quality and has a loop at the top to make sure the knife stays securely in its sheath when not in use. Never unsheathe your blade with your hand on the section of the sheath where the sharp edge lies, as the sheath may gradually wear away. Don't damage your knife by throwing or otherwise misusing it. It is your most important tool.

HOW TO SHARPEN YOUR KNIFE

To sharpen a knife with a stone, use granite, sandstone, or quartz. Granite is gray with a salt-and-pepper look and has crystalline features in it, while sandstone has a finer grain with smaller sand particles, making it easy to spot. Quartz is commonly found in its white or milky color.

PREPARING YOUR STONE

Ideally, choose rough and smooth pieces of stone for sharpening your knife. Rough stone can remove burrs and do the hard work of smoothing your knife, while a smoother-surfaced stone will sharpen it finely. You must wet the stones before you start. This will prevent the knife from dragging and developing burrs. Place the stone on a secure surface in front of you. Taking the handle in

Fig. 1—Rotate the blade clockwise across the stone as you push away

your right hand, put the fingers of your left hand on the blade and push away, moving the blade in a circular motion (clockwise as you push away).

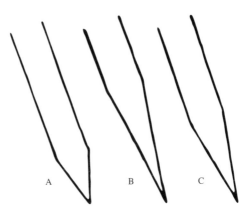

Fig. 2—The angle of the blade

THE ANGLE OF THE BLADE

Keep the angle of the blade to the stone at perhaps 20 degrees, paying attention to the blade before you begin. A smaller angle will create a very fine blade at the end, but this will chip (Fig. 2, example A).

A very flat, fine angle will make the blade thinner, but this will soon wear, as it is too narrow (Fig. 2, example B), while a gradual angle will last longer (Fig. 2, example C).

KEEPING YOUR KNIFE SHARP

A sharp knife will make your work easier. The knife is less likely to slip while you are using it and this actually makes it a safer knife. Getting into the habit of checking your gear and keeping track of all your tools and possessions is important on the journey, but keeping your knife functional is your priority.

8

USE A COMPASS, RADIO, AND GPS

When you are exploring, it is a good idea to know where you are and have the means to let others access this information should you be overtaken by dire circumstances. Learn how to use your compass, know how to use your radio, and understand how to interpret information from your GPS.

THE COMPASS

Ever noticed someone standing holding a compass while turning on the spot and then gazing about looking confused? To avoid this, follow these instructions.

First, look at your compass. You should be able to see a moving arrow that may be

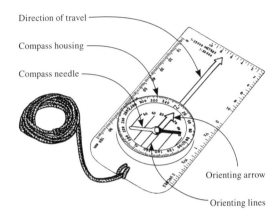

Direction of travel

Compass housing

Compass needle

Orienting arrow

Orienting lines

red and black. The red end of the arrow always points to magnetic north. There should also be lines, and an arrow called an orienting arrow, which points to true north.

This will be easier if you try it out with an actual map and compass. An orienteering compass enables you to determine an accurate direction of travel by lining up your compass with your map. If you have an orienteering compass with a rectangular base, there will be a directional arrow on this base. Place your compass on the map so that the directional arrow is pointing to your destination.

Turn the dial of the compass so that the orienting lines on the compass are in line with the vertical gridlines on the map. Do not move the compass on the map. What the compass needle says is north deviates from true north depending on the area you are traveling in. The map should indicate

whether to move the compass housing clockwise or counterclockwise, and by how many degrees to correct this magnetic variation. Make sure you are not carrying any iron, which will disturb the accuracy of the compass. Your compass is now aligned with your map.

Now, pick up your compass and turn yourself around until the red needle covers the orienting arrow so that the N of the needle is facing N on the compass. Stop. You are now facing the direction you wish to travel based on your current location and your chosen destination on the map.

This will not work if you do not know where you are or where you are going.

If you wish simply to head in a particular direction, and wish to know your bearing, then do the following. Lay the compass flat on your palm. Turn yourself so that you are facing the direction you wish to travel. Now, twist the compass housing so that the red compass needle and the orienting arrow align and point to N. Look at the compass to see what your bearing is. If it is between N and E, you will be traveling northeast. If the compass is between S and W, your bearing will be southwest. You should adjust the needle to account for magnetic variation. Consult your local map for the local deviation.

Check your bearing regularly. Regardless of how accurate you are at compass reading, there will be an error of two degrees to either side.

THE RADIO

It is possible, with the use of a compass and map, to pinpoint your position. Bringing a transmitter radio, which you use to contact a base radio, will allow you to update your contact person with your daily position. If you are traveling in harsh conditions, bad weather, or alone, this is highly recommended. You need to establish a contact time each day. Should you miss this time, your contact person will inform local police, mountain rescue, or other relevant authorities of your most recently reported position.

A radio contact person can also be used to keep you updated about local weather forecasts.

USE A GPS

A global positioning system (GPS) will, with about 95 percent accuracy, let you know where you are on the planet. If it has a digital display, it will even *show* you your location on a map. If you have the coordinates of your destination, it will plot a route for you to take. You can then get on your radio and let your contact know where you are.

But a word of caution is needed before you consider ditching your compass and

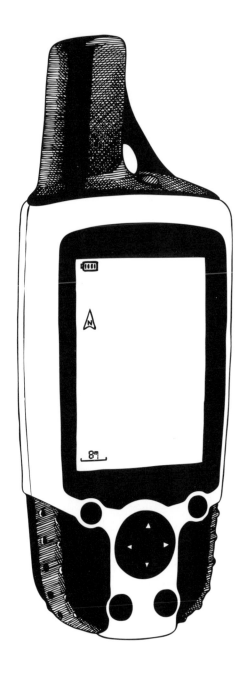

paper map. A GPS will only work if it can receive a signal, so you may need to head to high ground. It is battery-powered, so you need to make sure it is charged before you go. If you are not familiar with reading map coordinates, the information you receive may not be very helpful. A GPS is most useful if you can compare its information with your local map and plan your route accordingly, using your compass. The route the GPS suggests will not take into account the easiest way to hike and will not plan a trail that takes you past your ideal campsite.

9
READ A MAP

Map reading can be great fun and allows you to explore with confidence and arrive home safely afterward. Basic map reading ability should be a prerequisite for everyone in your group, and everyone should be made aware at regular intervals of where they are on the map. Try to avoid unpleasant scenes generated by being lost: arm waving, hair pulling, name calling, and unfortunate map tearing. You can best do this by assigning one person to be in charge of the map. If you are this person, you should read this section carefully.

FIND YOUR POSITION

Do you know where you are, and can you find that place on the map? If you are unsure of your location, look around you for obvious landmarks such as hills, mountains, rivers, or valleys. Pick two or three of these landmarks on either side of where you stand. Now consult your map, find these features, and estimate your position. Use your compass, or check the sun, to estimate north and compare this to the map (vertical gridlines on a map do not necessarily point north). This will ensure you are estimating your position on the correct side of the mountain. Do not consult the map first and then try to find the features it shows. This will get you lost.

SCALE AND DISTANCE

All maps will show scale. The most detailed will be a 1:50,000 scale. This is good for hiking. It should be noted that details such as rivers and roads are shown at a standard width, which may not be to scale. Also, when plotting your course, it is not always possible to travel in a straight line. If you are traveling in a straight line, you can simply compare the distance to the scale listed on the map. To estimate your distance, plot your course in a series of shorter straight lines, marked with points. Measure each line, add the measurements together, and compare to the scale. If you are traveling up any hill, you must add to your distance. The steeper the gradient, the more ground you will cover. For instance, a 45-degree gradient will add as much as 50 percent to the distance that is shown on the map.

COLORS AND FEATURES

You should familiarize yourself with the features that you may find listed on the map, and know which ones are shown to scale. Common features include hills, mountains, ravines, valleys, towns, roads, rivers, lakes, and railway tracks. Your map may come with a legend explaining the symbols. This should be referred to carefully, as maps in different countries vary in how they depict features. For example, a secondary road shown on a map in the United States would indicate a railway line on a map in Switzerland.

Colors also vary and can be misleading. Rivers are printed as blue and mountains as brown on most maps. Similarly, areas of dark green usually indicate areas at or below sea level, with white areas indicating high mountain peaks. Check the map legend for all explanations on the use of color. You should also note that a brown mountain on the map may be actually covered in trees, a green valley may be devoid of vegetation, and a blue river may be polluted.

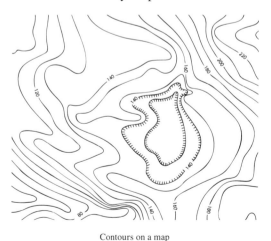

Contours on a map

CONTOURS

Reading contours on a map will help you avoid unwanted mountain treks and help you estimate distance.

Contours on a map depict the rise and fall of the land on paper. The shorter the distance between the contour lines, the steeper the incline. Numbers on the contour lines of the map will show height above sea level. If the numbers decrease toward the center, you are looking at a valley; if they increase, it is a hill or mountain.

MAGNETIC NORTH AND TRUE NORTH

All maps will have some indication of orientation that you should note. The vertical gridlines usually indicate north. Magnetic north—the north that is indicated by your compass—and geographic north are not exactly the same. The variance between them is referred to as declination. The extent of the declination depends on where you are and what year it is. In the United States, if you are traveling along the Mississippi River, for instance, there is no declination. Elsewhere you may need to alter your compass by 10 degrees east. A map will indicate the declination for the region and for the year it was printed. It will also estimate the rate of change for each year. These estimates of change are very often wrong, so new or very recent maps of the area are essential.

PLOTTING COORDINATES

When you are reading a map, you will notice that there are numbers on both the horizontal and vertical edges of the page. These numbers show coordinates. Mark your position on the map. Now, draw a horizontal and a vertical line from your position to the sides of the map. If your map gives details of latitude and longitude, you will then be able to accurately state, with the use of numbers, where you are. The greater the number of digits, the more detailed the map and the greater the accuracy of your information.

If your map simply shows a grid reference for that map, usually a mixture of letters and numbers, that is an ordinance survey reference that can be converted into latitude and longitude references with some complex math. Either will suffice for your map reading, or if you need to radio your position for rescue. Always state the horizontal numbers (longitude) first, followed by the vertical numbers (latitude). Do not include spaces (e.g., 30 West longitude and 22 North latitude = 3022).

10
SELECT A CAMPSITE

What makes a good campsite? This of course will vary depending on the climate, terrain, and the size of your group. Regardless of where you are, you want to find somewhere safe, sheltered, and flat, with good drainage, a supply of firewood, and relatively near fresh, clean water.

WATER

Ideally, you want to camp about 200 feet (60 meters) from water. Any closer and you run the risk of flooding your tent or obstructing the wildlife's access to the water. Water is essential for drinking, cooking, washing, and cleaning. The farther away it is, the more work it will be to carry it to your campsite. Water also means flies and mosquitoes.

This is unavoidable. Your campfire, some good repellent, and a light breeze may help.

If you are on a beach, staying close to the water is not necessarily a good plan. The high tide line indicates where the sea will reach at high tide. Above this, you may find greenery and very dry sand or soil, but you will not find seaweed, seashells, or other debris from the sea. Camp above this line and avoid getting wet.

OTHER CAMPERS

If your expedition is in popular camping territory, you should be aware that not all areas permit camping. Try to get information about known campsites where you will be traveling. This will save you time, as known campsites will probably be nice, dry, flat areas that are sheltered and near water. Other campers may object to you settling in next door or obscuring their mountain view, so if possible find a spot out of earshot of others. If you are on a well-worn trail, try to find a spot 200 feet (60 meters) away from it so you are not disturbed by passersby.

SHELTER

If you are setting up an emergency camp in the hopes of being rescued, you will want to stay visible. If not, head for a nice sheltered spot. Trees, bushes, cacti, or rocks will do the trick. The base of a hill may seem sheltered, but could also expose you to flooding. Low-lying areas are colder at night and damper in the morning.

If you are camping for more than one night, try to find a spot where your tent will not be heated by the midday sun.

In winter, slightly higher ground will be warmer. Calculate where the morning sun will shine and pitch your tent there. This may help get you out of your cozy sleeping bag.

BE SAFE

The desire for privacy and shelter should always be measured against the need to be safe. Trees and rocks may provide shade and a nice windbreak. They may also shelter snakes or prevent you from seeing the approach of dangerous predators. Taking time to go away from used trails to find a hidden spot is only a good idea if you are in a group and have a means of signaling for help.

Check around your chosen campsite for any sign of other residents—animal or human—who may already be living there, or partially uprooted trees that may blow down on top of you.

WHAT DO YOU NEED?

You have determined that you are safe, near water, and sheltered. The area needs to be big enough to allow all your tents to be erected, to allow you to have a fire, and to allow you to provide a designated area for food storage and preparation. Assign a tree limb to hang any food, and another tree limb for drying clothes. Find an area for your campfire and ensure there is space nearby to store your fuel. Make sure there is a good six-foot (two-meter) area around the fire so that you have room to place logs or other seating.

If you are near your water source, but the view to it is obscured, you will want to mark a trail to it. You will also need to find a suitable spot for your camp latrine that is downwind from your tents and away from your water supply. A very clear trail to the latrine will enable visits in the dark so you don't have to hold out until dawn.

11
ERECT A TENT

TRY IT OUT

The light is fading rapidly, rain is approaching, and you are exhausted from the day's uphill hike, hungry, and beset by mosquitoes. Now, unpack your new tent and commence reading the instructions, which are badly translated from Japanese. If this sounds like an unappealing prospect, then practice before you set out on your expedition. Pick a calm, sunny afternoon outside your home as you sip a cold beverage. You may of course be beset by neighborhood children trying to jump in and claim the tent as their clubhouse.

THINGS TO AVOID

Do not pitch your tent on a slope or on boggy or rocky ground. Try to find a relatively sheltered spot. Spend time securing all pegs into the ground. Replacing them in the middle of the night is not much fun. Making sure the tent material is taut will prevent noisy flapping if the wind should pick up during the night. Do not face the door of your tent toward the prevailing wind. Use a tent that fits the environment and the size of the party. A tent for two campers should be big enough to allow you both to sit up and to store both backpacks at night as you sleep. A two-man tent is only really suitable for one man and his equipment. A party of four will need at least a five-man tent. Do not lean or place any equipment against the sides of your tent, as this may cause water to seep in.

BEFORE YOU BUY YOUR TENT

There are some simple questions you should ask yourself before purchasing your tent. There are many styles and sizes to choose from, and prices vary widely. To prevent overspending or buying unusable equipment, think about these things:

- Is the tent easy to put up? Large, cheap ones can be difficult to erect. Pop-up tents tend not to be robust.
- Is it suitable for hot/cold/stormy weather?
- How heavy is it to carry when folded, and is it possible to hike with it? The average fit person can only carry about 25 pounds (11 kilograms) and hike for a day.
- Is it robust and can you get replacement parts later?
- How spacious is it inside?
- How much does it cost?

PITCH YOUR TENT

There are some tents that you simply unwrap and throw in the air, they pop up, and then you peg in the line to secure them to the ground. Other styles that are simple to erect include inflatable ones, for which you need an electric pump, or "instant tents," which have a skeleton of poles permanently fixed into the fabric.

Let's assume that you have a slightly more challenging tent. Take note of the direction of the wind and erect your tent so that it backs toward the wind and any rain that may follow. Unroll the tent and lay it out in your chosen pitching site. Read and follow the instructions carefully. While it is possible to erect many tents alone, it is much quicker if you have a group. Secure the guy ropes and temporarily fix the side pegs. Climb inside the tent and fix all the poles into position. Now, go around your tent and reposition all your outside pegs. If possible, have another person work on the opposite side of the tent in order to get perfect tension. Drive pegs into the ground at an angle downward and pointing in toward the tent.

WINDY WEATHER

If the weather is stormy or windy, you will have difficulty erecting your tent. The trick is to lie on top of your tent as you unroll it. Now, preferably with the help of someone else, drive the pegs into the ground while keeping as much of your body on the tent as possible. Fix the guy ropes. Only when this is done can you risk climbing inside the tent and putting up the poles. Stow all of your equipment inside and go outside to secure all of the pegs again. To make your tent more secure in inclement weather, place rocks or mound some snow around—but not touching—three sides of your tent.

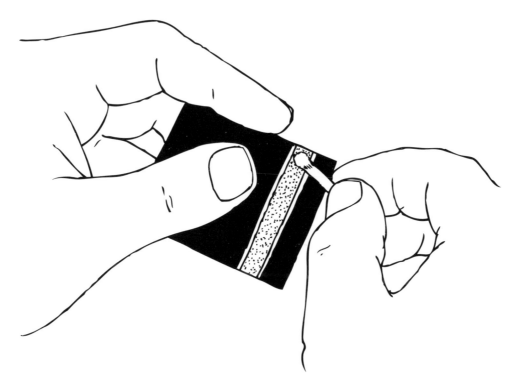

12
LIGHT A FIRE

WHY BOTHER

In order to be properly motivated before undertaking this task, you may wish to consider all the ways fire will be beneficial. Of course, it is fun making fire. It will also keep you warm, allow you to purify water, cook, dry your clothes, make smoke signals and get rescued, melt ice, scare away predators, repel insects, and help you see around your camp.

MATCHES

If you have packed well, you will have matches to light your fire. The more enterprising may also have packed some flint. The extremely well-organized adventurer will have some soft cotton soaked in gasoline and stored in an airtight container, thereby removing the need to search for dry tinder.

OTHER MEANS

Have you no matches and have you mislaid your flint? Happily there are other means of creating the initial fire-lighting spark. Do you wear glasses? If it is a sunny day, simply use your glasses to focus a beam of sunlight onto some prepared dry tinder. This can also work using a magnifying glass or camera lens. A condom or balloon may also be partially filled with water and squeezed into an appropriate shape to allow a beam of sunlight to focus. This will need to be held close to the tinder.

If it is not sunny and you are carrying ammunition, open a round and sprinkle some of the gunpowder onto your tinder. Any small spark will easily light it. If you have a car battery, connect wires to both points and touch these together to create a spark.

MORE PRIMITIVE METHODS

More primitive methods of fire making require more skill, time, and practice, but are quite rewarding when successful. Any hard stone and piece of steel banged together will make a spark eventually, but it may take a while to get your tinder to light. Making a bow drill is a surer method, but it requires work and persistence.

MAKE A FIRE DRILL

• **Drill**. The drill is a straight, hardwood stick about three quarters of an inch (two

centimeters) in diameter and 10 inches (25 centimeters) long.

• **Socket**. Find a fist-sized stone or piece of hardwood or bone with a slight depression in one side. You will use this on top of the drill to hold it in place and to apply downward pressure.

• **Fire board**. A softwood board that is about an inch (two and a half centimeters) thick and four inches (10 centimeters) wide, but you can be flexible with the size.

• **Bow**. The bow is a strong green stick about an inch (two and a half centimeters) in diameter with a string attached. Any type of wood or string that is available can be used. Simply tie the bowstring from one end of the bow to the other, ensuring there is no slack.

Cut up to three depressions about three quarters of an inch (two centimeters) from the edge on one side of the board. On the underside, make a V-shaped cut from the edge of the board to the depression.

HOW TO USE
THE BOW AND DRILL

- Place tinder under one of the V-shaped grooves.
- Place one foot on the fire board to steady it.
- Loop the bowstring over the drill and place the drill in the precut depression on the fire board above the tinder.
- Place the socket on the top of the drill to hold it in position. Press down on the drill and move the bow back and forth. Now, apply more downward pressure and work the bow faster.

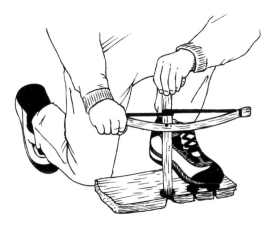

How to use the bow and drill

- This action will grind hot black powder into the tinder, hopefully causing a spark to catch. Blow on the tinder until it ignites.

13
RUN AN EFFICIENT CAMP

DISCIPLINE

It is important for someone to be in charge in order for a camp to run efficiently. This could be you. Everyone needs to be given tasks, and if you are in charge it will be your happy duty to assign them. Each night you should discuss who will undertake tasks for the next day. You may need to allow a certain amount of democratic discussion.

TASKS

Daily tasks should include the collection of water, firewood, and tinder; maintenance of the fire; cooking and cleaning; airing out tents and bedding; and setting and checking traps. Other tasks will include food rationing, hunting, fishing, foraging, and preparing game. You may also wish to include camp crafts, like building shelters or seating, digging a latrine, and making tools and weapons.

HYGIENE

Keeping yourself and your camp clean will not only endear you to your fellow campers, it will also help you stay healthy. Finding a place to bathe and to clean clothes and establishing this routine in camp is essential. Dirty hands can lead to the spread of bacteria. Fleas, lice, and other parasites can take up residence in clothes, hair, or bedding. Each day sleeping bags should be turned inside out and aired. If water is in short supply and clothes cannot be washed, try to air them out. Always wear clean underwear and socks.

ROUTINE

Routine will aid efficiency. Establish a time when everyone rises and a time in the morning for certain tasks. Cleaning is best done in the morning when you have a full day's sunshine for drying. Hunting is also best at this time. Foraging and trap checking can be done in the late afternoon. Assign tasks based on each person's age, fitness, competence, and interest. One person given responsibility for collecting firewood every day may lose motivation, thus reducing camp efficiency.

STAY ACTIVE

Staying active will prevent boredom, depression, and stress in camp. If bad weather or an emergency has stranded you in one place, establishing a routine may be essential for survival. Getting up and moving in the morning will help maintain a positive attitude in camp and also ensure that all the important tasks get completed in daylight.

SOLITARY CAMPING

If you are camping alone, deciding who will complete each task will be less problematic, but there are other barriers to efficiency. Isolation and loneliness may lead to depression and a lack of motivation. A change in weather may lead to uncomfortable conditions and create more work. Stay positive and focused. Plan each day and know what tasks you need to prioritize.

AN EFFICIENT CAMP IS A SAFE CAMP

Routines and the undertaking of essential tasks should not be ignored. A lack of firewood, shortage of food or water, or lapse in hygiene could have serious consequences. Hunger, thirst, illness, and hypothermia may be the result of not running an efficient camp.

So, stagger into your tidy tent and out of your clean socks into your well-aired, louse-free sleeping bag. You are safe in the knowledge that the fire is lit, the latrine is covered, and the food is safely stored. You can sleep happily until dawn, when the next day's chores await you.

BOOK TWO

ENJOYING THE OUTDOORS

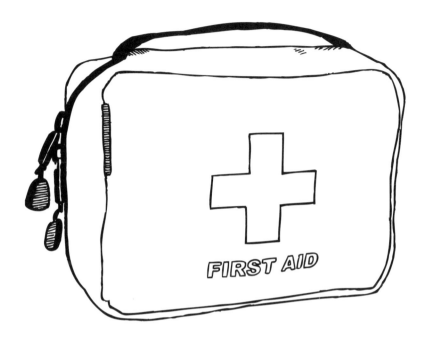

14
ENJOY THE OUTDOORS SAFELY

Take the proper precautions to ensure that you stay safe and healthy on your excursion.

THE SUN

Avoid dehydration and sunburn. Carry enough water for your trip and bring purification tablets in case you run out of the water you brought. Wear long-sleeved, light-colored, cool clothing, a hat, and sunglasses. Make sure to coat your skin in sunscreen. It is possible to burn skin in the shade and even through clothing. At high altitude in the winter, the sun can cause severe eye damage and burn your skin by reflecting off snow and ice, so sunscreen and sunglasses are a must.

INSECTS

Wearing insect repellent can protect you from mosquitoes and other biting insects. It will also dissuade ticks and leeches from attaching to your skin. Tucking pants into socks and wearing long-sleeved tops will also help. If possible, avoid walking through swamps and long, dense foliage. Check your skin frequently for ticks, as quick removal will prevent you from catching Lyme disease or other infections.

WATCH YOUR FEET

Keep a careful watch where you walk to avoid stepping on insects, spiders, or snakes. Wear hard-soled shoes to protect you from bites and stings or cuts from sharp roots and growing plants. Never place your feet or hands into any dark crevice, hollow log, murky water, or rock pool.

FIRST AID

Pack a suitable first aid kit that takes account of the number of people in the group, the length of your expedition or hike, and the region of the world you are in. At a bare minimum, you should ensure you have analgesic, antibiotic, diarrhea treatment, water sterilization tablets, Band-Aids, butterfly sutures, a scalpel, and some soap or hand sanitizer. At least one person in the group should be well versed in first aid.

CLOTHING

The season, region, and weather forecast should dictate your clothing. Proper footwear is essential both for comfort and protection. Clothing should be practical, durable, and comfortable. Natural fibers will allow for better air circulation and will dry quicker if you get wet. A large waterproof poncho may prove useful to protect you from a sudden downpour or even to fashion a makeshift shelter.

STAY IN CONTACT

Always carry a map of the area and make sure you are able to read it. A GPS allows you to pinpoint your position with accuracy. A transmitter radio is a good idea if you are planning a longer expedition to a remote area so that you can stay in contact and get weather updates. If you are somewhere less remote, bring your cell phone to stay in touch and enable you to call for help. Make sure to notify someone of your plans and your route before you leave. Make a contingency plan in case of a medical emergency or other mishap, and ensure that everyone traveling with you—as well as your contact people at home—know the plan. In each area you travel, you should establish a rendezvous point in case you lose someone.

STAY WARM

Never suck ice in cold climates, as it will lead to hypothermia. In order to use ice for drinking, you need first to use a fire to melt it. Always avoid getting wet unnecessarily, and quickly remove wet clothing and replace it with dry. Remember, even deserts become cold at night, and warm clothing and a fire are essential.

15
IDEAS FOR FURNISHING YOUR CAMP

Your camp will seem more homey and comfortable if you furnish it with some seats, a bed, and even a lamp or some rustic cooking utensils.

A SEAT

A seat is a good place to rest your weary bones and to keep you off the damp ground. Of course, a well-placed rock or felled tree will work if it is already conveniently placed in your camp. If you are not that lucky, simply find four logs at least the thickness of your leg and higher than your knee. Cut so that they are the same length. Lash two pairs together in an X shape. Lay a fifth log across the top. Test to make sure it holds your weight. Experiment with different sizes. For extra comfort, you may wish to consider splitting the log used as the seat.

A BED

A bed will help keep you dry, warm, and away from crawling insects. First, find four strong pieces of wood and make two A-frames by lashing them together and securing the posts into the ground. Create a ladder with two long, sturdy poles joined by lashing smaller pieces horizontally across. This ladder will sit over the A-frame

support. Now, lay branches and leaves on top of your ladder to make a mattress.

If you want a lazier solution, simply lay pine branches in layers on the ground, alternating the direction of the branches until you achieve a comfortable-looking bed.

Another easy solution is to find two or more long, wide logs, longer than you are tall. Lay them side by side. Your bed should be about three feet (one meter) wide. Drive four stakes into the ground on both sides of the logs so that they are unable to roll. Layer leafy branches, leaves, and twigs on the logs until they feel soft. A pillow may be fashioned from dry leaves.

CONTAINERS

Make your own bowls using bone, horn, bark, or wood. Simply hollow out or form your material into the desired shape using your knife or some tools you have fashioned from stone or bone.

Strips of birch bark can be curled into a cone shape. Then, tie string around the cone shape to stop it from unraveling. If you suspend this with string over a fire, you can use it to boil water safely.

Cooking bowls may be made from wood. Ensure the bowl hangs over the fire high enough to prevent it from burning. Use clean stones that are not cracked or hollow and place them next to the fire. Carefully pick up the stones when they are hot and put them into your wooden bowl with the water and food you are cooking. Continually replace the stones with hot ones from next to the fire. The stones will make the food cook quicker than simply suspending the pot over the fire.

Turtle shells can be put directly onto the fire for cooking. A coconut shell or a seashell can be hung over the fire to boil water in and cook food, or can be used as a cup.

Bamboo can be fashioned into excellent pots, cups, and bowls. If you are using bamboo for cooking, first cut a piece of bamboo about two feet (60 centimeters) long. Then, cut out a section in the center about 10 inches (25 centimeters) long and five inches (12 centimeters) wide. You can make your cut bigger if your bamboo is very thick. Place your food and water into this opening. Lay the bamboo over the fire, placing it on stick supports you have made. Rocks placed on both sides of the fire can be used as props to hold the bamboo pot over the fire. You want to create a distance of about six inches (15 centimeters) between the bottom of your pot and the fire.

Be warned that bamboo that is left uncut along the seam will explode when heated and cause serious injury, which may spoil your dinner.

TORCHES

Make torches and lamps by tying used tin cans to wooden or metal poles, and filling the cans with oil.

UTENSILS

Spoons, knives, and forks can also be fashioned for your camp. Ensure that you use a type of wood that does not ooze syrup or sap. Oak, birch, and hardwood trees are good for this purpose. Bamboo is also ideal. Simply sit at your leisure on your newly fashioned seat and whittle your chosen wood into the desired shape. Always work by moving the knife away from yourself to prevent accidental stabbings.

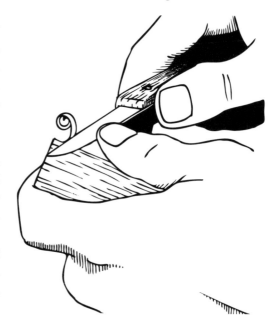

16
TAKE A SAFE SWIM

Swimming in the wilds has become a popular pastime for many, in both the sea and other bodies of water.

PRECAUTIONS

Before you take your dip, here are some good questions to ask yourself:

- Will I be swimming with alligators, sharks, or other dangerous fish or animals?
- Is the water clean and free of weeds or algae?
- Is there a strong current or undertow?
- Are there rocks or obstructions that may cause me injury?
- Do locals swim here and consider it safe?
- If I run into difficulty, will anyone rescue me?

If you are swimming alone in deep water, consider tying an inflatable around your ankle to increase your buoyancy. It is best to pick a known safe place, free of sharp rocks, with clear, clean water, manageable currents or waves, and devoid of predatory animals. It is also best to swim with others or at least in view of someone who can save you should the unexpected occur.

THE UNEXPECTED

You could be stung, bitten, or attacked. You could suffer from cramps. You could be carried away by a current. You could be sucked under a wave. You could suffer from hypothermia. You could be trapped in weeds. Do not let these possibilities frighten you away from the water. Simply take the following steps and your next swim need not be your last.

STUNG, BITTEN, OR ATTACKED

If you are approached by an alligator or crocodile, get out of the water immediately. You must avoid being clamped in its jaws if at all possible. If it grabs one of your limbs, hit it on the nose to get it to open its mouth. Seek medical attention immediately.

If you are bitten by a snake, get out of the water. If possible, tie something a few inches (centimeters) above the bite to avoid the poison spreading to your heart and brain. Wash the bite with soap and water. Do not cut the wound or let anyone try to suck out the venom. Use a suction cup. Seek medical attention quickly. Try to remain calm, as this will slow the spread of the venom. Try to get a good description of the snake so

that the appropriate antivenom can be given to you. Bites, even from nonvenomous snakes, can induce an allergic reaction or cause infection, so they should always be treated seriously.

All stings from fish or shellfish should be treated like a snakebite.

If you get stung by a jellyfish, do not touch the bite. Wipe the area with sand or cloth to remove any tentacles and avoid further stings. Wash the area with hot water immediately.

If you are unfortunate enough to be attacked by a shark, attack its eyes and gills with whatever you have to hand or use your hands. Try to persuade the shark that you are not an easy meal. Do not punch the shark. If you see sharks approaching, try to swim away with an even, unhurried stroke. Excessive splashing in the water may persuade them that you are prey.

Electric eels or piranhas may join you if you swim in South America. Try to avoid them. Leeches may live in rivers or lakes in all warm climates. Best to keep your eyes open and your mouth closed if you suspect them to be nearby.

CAUGHT IN A CURRENT

Try to determine the strength of a river current by throwing a stick into the water. If it moves faster than you can swim or if there are any indications that countercurrents are moving below the surface, swim elsewhere. Think ahead. Look downstream or check out the shoreline to ensure there are safe places to leave the water if you get carried downstream.

Do not attempt to swim against a current. You will tire yourself out and not get very far. Swim in a sidestroke diagonally to the direction of the current and make for the shore farther downstream.

CARRIED UNDER BY A WAVE

If you are swimming in the sea and the waves are large, always stay within your depth. If you spot a large wave approaching you, turn to face it, then sink under the water until the wave has passed. If you get pulled under or tossed by the wave, allow yourself to sink so that you can push your feet off of the seabed and reach the surface. If you are spun around by a wave and become disoriented, allow some air to escape from your mouth. The resulting bubble will float upward, showing which way is up. Swim back to shore once you break the surface and signal for help by shouting and waving.

ROCKS AND WEEDS

Do not swim in any river or pond that is full of rocks or in the sea where rocks are present. Cuts, bruises, fractures, or concussions could occur. Currents or unexpected waves may make avoiding such obstacles impossible once in the water.

If you find yourself in a body of water full of weeds, do not try to swim away vigorously because you will risk entanglement. Instead, float on your back and allow the current to take you away, or you can gently paddle away with your arms. Alternatively, change your direction very slowly, and once you are clear, swim away.

CRAMPS AND HYPOTHERMIA

Stomach cramps may occur if you eat too soon before swimming or undertaking any strenuous exercise. Swimmer's cramp is more likely to occur due to fatigue, overexertion, or dehydration and will occur in your calf or foot.

If you suffer from cramp, turn to float on your back and shout for help. Shouting will be more effective if you are not alone. Then, using your arms, start to slowly paddle back to the shoreline or shallow water.

Hypothermia can occur in outdoor swimming because water saps the body of heat very quickly. If your teeth start chattering and you start shivering, get out of the water, as these are the first stages of hypothermia. Put on warm clothes and commence jogging or doing jumping jacks to warm up. If you jump into cold water, your body may go into "cold shock," which will result in a rise in your heart rate. Get out of the water and warm yourself as quickly as possible.

Avoid all this unpleasantness by swimming in warmer water, wearing a wet suit, and gradually walking into the water, which will acclimate you to the temperature.

DISEASES AND ALGAE

Not all water is suitable for swimming. If you are concerned about the water quality, it is best to find somewhere else to swim. If you are determined to swim, ensure that all open cuts are carefully covered in waterproof Band-Aids and keep your mouth, nose, and eyes out of the water. Should you suffer from flu or jaundice-like symptoms after such a swim, seek medical attention, as you may need antibiotics to rid yourself of unwanted bacteria.

If you notice that the water is covered in algae or you come across water covered in green scum, try to avoid swimming through it. Algae can cause skin and eye irritations or make you ill if you swallow it.

Marshy, swampy, or stagnant water should always be avoided, as these types of water may harbor unseen residents. Leeches are fond of such water. Snails living in stagnant water can cause extreme skin irritation. Bacteria in such water can also cause illness.

17
TAKE GOOD OUTDOOR PHOTOGRAPHS

The ability to capture the beauty of the great outdoors will enhance your experience and enable you to share it with others you know and love. If your journey allows you to take good photographic equipment, ensure that you have the ability to safely store and transport the gear, and that you understand your terrain; specialist equipment for the outdoors is essential when you are traveling in demanding terrain.

PLANNING
Planning your route will give you the ability to plan your photography. The season may dictate possibilities with regard to wildlife in the area, and you will be aware of the weather conditions expected and can plan to take advantage of them as you enjoy the terrain and its visual possibilities. There is usually much birdlife on show, unless you are in extreme terrain and depending somewhat on the season. Many animals will not stray far from main water sources, so being near the water is an opportunity for you to capture local wildlife on camera.

TIME OF DAY
Outdoor photos are influenced mainly by the time of day. The light of dusk is perfect for certain landscapes, such as seascapes, which take on magnificent colors as light from the sun diminishes. Similarly, it would be a shame

to pass through an impressive valley or other far-reaching view late in the day when heavy shadows rob the scene of its beauty.

Before sunrise is an interesting time to take photographs because of the "bluish" color that can precede sunrise. There is a bright but shadowless light before sunrise occurs that is useful for most outdoor photography.

Sunrise and *sunset* are useful for high contrast pictures of the sky, landscape, and silhouettes, if you have the right view. The colors can also be an amazing addition to your landscape, which you can include by getting up early or taking up your position before sunset. You should avoid shooting toward the sun unless it is rising or setting, as the exposure will be extreme and drown out your images.

Mornings and *afternoons* are useful times for all outdoor photography, because the light of the sun is bright but not dazzling, giving the photographer a good chance of shooting wildlife or a landscape. Afternoons provide a similar light, but offer a warmer color to your photographs as the sun begins its retreat.

Noon is probably not the time to be taking landscape photographs if the sun is out, as the light is at its most powerful, drowning out the other colors in images. However, it can be a good time for photographing wildlife.

Evening and particularly *dusk* are perfect times for rich, unexpected colors, particularly

if you can set your camera for a long exposure, and can capture these changing colors, which are not all visible to the human eye.

TAKING PHOTOGRAPHS OF WILDLIFE

If you are shooting wildlife with a camera, it helps immensely to have an adjustable telephoto lens that allows you to zoom up to 300 millimeters, since you cannot control the subject and it will be difficult to get close to it. Set your camera at its widest aperture (consult the camera's manual), letting the most light in for the wildlife photos. Don't be disheartened by how difficult it is. If you have time, observe spots where wildlife gathers, such as a popular watering hole, and get closer to await your opportunity. If you have the ability to do this on a fine day, you can consider leaving your camera in a prime location and letting it automatically take pictures at set intervals to see what you can capture. The risk of someone stealing your equipment must be kept in mind, of course.

18
OBSERVE AND COLLECT NATURALIST SPECIMENS

Collecting plants and other specimens has been an occupation of explorers and adventurers since at least the nineteenth century. Most explorers collected specimens in order to fund their expeditions. Many of these early travelers and botanists, sadly, died on their travels.

Miltonia cultivar

PLANT HUNTING

Plant hunting is the term used to describe collecting live plant specimens in the wild.

An herbarium is a collection of plants, or parts of plants, in a dried form for reference and identification, usually mounted on a card or in an album. Most collectors of live plants look for specific species and then house them in their own gardens and greenhouses. Collectors most often seek out orchids, roses, and cultivars—a general term for plants chosen for their ornamental appeal. If you wish to take a live plant home, remove a sample, preferably with its roots, and a small amount of soil.

ILLEGAL TRANSPORT

There are 25,000 known species of orchids found in the wild and another 60,000 hybrid species created by collectors. Many wild orchid varieties are threatened with extinction due to habitat destruction and illegal poaching. Orchids are found in nearly every habitat on earth, although many commercially sold orchids come from the tropics. If you come across certain varieties, you should be aware that attempting to travel with any species of orchid that is considered endangered—or its seeds—could result in prosecution. Before you collect any plant life, make sure you check out whether this is permitted in the area you are traveling in.

COLLECTING YOUR SAMPLE

Before you set out, ensure you have a notebook and pencil to record the details of your find, some sealable plastic bags, and a small knife for trimming. When you find a plant you wish to collect, record where you are, giving details as to shade, and, if possible, the surrounding plant life. Record the date. The same plant may look different in the spring than the autumn. Take as complete a sample as possible, preferably including the root. Choose a healthy specimen that has not been squashed or eaten. Take care that no insect life is living in your specimen. Place in your bag. Seeds may be collected from unprotected species and kept in dry, airtight containers. These can then be planted in your garden.

PRESSING YOUR SAMPLE

Use a plant press to quickly dry your plant for attractive display in your album. If you do not have a press, you can make one by arranging your plant between layers of clean tissue. Place the tissue inside a book.

Lay the book on the ground and place as many heavy logs or rocks as you can on top. Attempt to apply even pressure. You may also sit on the book or place it under you while you sleep.

TAKE PICTURES

Many collectors have switched from keeping albums of dried plants, with descriptions of the time and place they are found, to taking digital photographs. These can then be compiled into a digital album, and printed, distributed, and shared. If you are interested in plants and wish to create an herbarium, you should consider at least backing up your find by also taking a photograph.

MAKING A DISCOVERY

Should you feel confident that you have discovered a *new* plant, collect and preserve a sample. This can then be sent to a botanical garden, such as Kew Gardens in London, England. They will verify if it is in fact previously unrecorded and then classify and name the plant. If you also bring back viable seeds from a plant, you can be credited with a new plant "introduction," in addition to a new plant "discovery."

INSECTS, FLIES, AND SPIDERS

If you wish to collect other specimens, you should still record details in your notebook, as with plant collecting. Small insects or worms can be stored in empty, clean medicine bottles. Airtight lunch boxes can be used for larger specimens, such as spiders, scorpions, or amphibians. It is not advisable to keep *live* specimens of any animals or insects in containers, as the lack of oxygen may kill them. Some species of frogs are considered endangered. Many countries will not allow you to cross its borders with any samples of wildlife. Check these rules carefully to avoid confiscation or prosecution.

19
EXPLORE AND KEEP YOUR BEARINGS

A compass and a map should be part of every adventurer's equipment. Once you have discovered where you are on your map and know where you are headed, your adventure has begun. It is reassuring, while exploring, to feel confident that you are on course and will in fact arrive at the desired destination. A compass is a very convenient tool, as it will give you an accurate reading of what direction you are moving in. Simply compare this with the direction of north indicated on your map and you will know which direction to head in.

- Then, carefully press the needle into the piece of cork so that it sticks out each side evenly.
- Fill a glass or other container half full of water so that the cork can float freely.
- Ensure the container is resting on a flat surface.
- The needle will point to the nearest magnetic pole, north or south, depending on whether you are in the Northern or Southern Hemisphere.
- You will need to re-magnetize your needle occasionally.

MAKE YOUR OWN COMPASS

If you have no compass or map, there are ways of remaining on course. The best way is to make your own compass. Follow these simple directions.

You will need a sewing needle, a magnet, a bowl, and a piece of cork.
- First, rub the needle against the magnet in one direction. This will magnetize the needle.

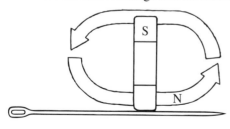

If you lack a cork or suitable container, simply magnetize the needle and suspend it with a thread from its center with a steady hand until it stops spinning. If you do not have a magnet, rub the needle against silk in one direction. If you have no cork or thread, lay the magnetized needle on a piece of thin paper or foam in the water.

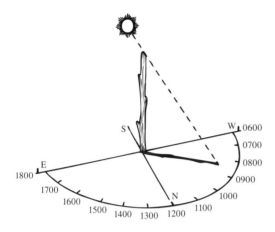

STICK AND THE SUN

If you have no needle or suitable alternative, you can use the sun. Find a flat, sunny spot and bury a straight 18-inch (45-centimeter) stick so that its top stands 12 inches (30 centimeters) from the ground. First thing in the morning, place a stone where the stick's shadow falls. About 12 hours later, place another stone where the shadow has moved. The halfway point, or where the shadow falls at midday, will face *south* in the Northern Hemisphere or *north* in the Southern Hemisphere. This compass is rather stationary. It is best to find a large object in the distance, such as a mountain, see where it lies with respect to your newly determined south (or north), and use this object or mountain to plot your course as you travel. You can repeat your stick compass exercise at your next camp.

MAKE YOUR OWN MAP

If you are without a map but have paper and pencil, then consider making your own map. Find a spot on high ground with a good view of the surroundings. Draw a basic map showing any hills, rivers, or notable landmarks, such as distinctive tree clusters or waterfalls. Try to keep things in scale: If the trees are twice the distance from the river as the hills are, show this on your map. Use the position of the sun to determine the direction of north. If you are in the Northern Hemisphere and it is midday and you are facing the sun, you are facing south. Do the same thing in the Southern Hemisphere and you will be facing north. Add to the map as you travel. It may be helpful to mark out any animal lairs, sources of water, or good camping spots as you go. If you are forced to turn back, or plan to have future excursions in the area, you will have a very useful map.

USE NATURE
TO POINT YOUR WAY

Plants grow toward the sun, especially flowering plants. In the Northern Hemisphere, plants and trees will grow more abundantly on the southern side of a hill. The opposite is true in the Southern Hemisphere. This may help keep you on course as you travel.

WIND

If you are traveling in a coastal area, it is helpful to know that wind generally blows inland off any large body of water during the day. If you know that the sea or nearby lake lies to the west, you can determine your direction even if you can't see the sea or lake, because the daytime breeze off a body of water will usually come from that direction.

If you are traveling in an area with a naturally occurring prevailing wind direction, use this information as a guide to your direction of travel.

Since weather and winds frequently change, it is best to use wind direction as a guide only in conjunction with other signs, such as plant life and position of the sun.

20
READ THE WEATHER SIGNS

Weather can change rapidly and tends to be localized. Knowing the expected average temperature during the season and within the region you are traveling will help you pack. Daily and hourly weather updates can be very helpful in deciding when to hike, when to make camp, or when to make dinner to avoid the torrential downpour that is due. It is possible to use your surroundings and your senses to make good, accurate assessments of the weather.

CLOUDS

Looking at the sky is a well-used method of attempting to forecast the weather. There are many types of clouds and not all cloudy days result in rain. Some clouds are actually an indication of continuing good weather.

As a general rule, if the clouds are white, fluffy, high in the sky, and well spaced, it will not rain. If the clouds are low down, dark, and thick, or in large clusters, rain is imminent.

If you see a large bank of dark clouds forming an anvil shape, it is an indication of heavy rain, possibly with thunder and lightning. If the clouds are like a wide gray veil, rain is on its way. If the clouds are low on the hills and it is misty but there is no wind, it will probably not rain.

RED SKY

The saying, "A red sky at night is a sailor's delight," has merit. If sunset results in a brilliant red sky, then the next day will be dry and fine, for at least the first few hours after dawn. A similar red sky at dawn is a sign of approaching rain.

AIR PRESSURE

A change in the weather is usually preceded by a change in air pressure. Some people with rheumatism claim to be able to predict rain by the increased pains in their inflamed joints. Other signs of changes in air pressure can be seen by looking at your campfire. If the smoke rises in a steady way, the weather will remain the same, but if the smoke begins to swirl or descend, it indicates the low pressure that precedes bad weather.

ANIMALS

Animals are sensitive to changes in air pressure. You may notice swallows or other insect-eating birds flying lower to the ground when bad weather is coming. If the birds are flying high in the sky, the weather should remain fine. Butterflies will suddenly disappear from view just before rainfall. Animals may behave in an erratic way or stray from their usual habits before a storm. Nocturnal animals may be noticed foraging during the daylight hours when bad weather is on its way. You might notice rats running around your campsite during the day. This is a sign that you need to reconsider your camp hygiene and prepare for bad weather—once you climb down off your campstool.

WIND

Changes in the wind will be a good indication of a change in the weather. Strong dry winds coming from one direction will not carry rain. If this type of wind persists, it is a sign that the weather will probably remain dry. If it is foggy and then becomes windy, it may rain. A sudden increase in the wind is an indication of a change in the weather. On a fine, dry day any noticeable increase in wind could herald rain.

21
TELL THE TIME BY THE SUN

HOW TO TELL THE TIME BY THE SUN—SUN POSITION METHOD

In an unfamiliar environment, finding out what time it is may be a matter of safety and survival. If you are in the wilderness as the sun starts to wane, you may find it quite useful to know how much time you have before sunset. Finding the exact time may not be possible, but you can figure out the approximate time using the sun. We're looking now at the sun position method.

GETTING STARTED

First, you need to decide on the position of the sun. For that, you need to act based on the hemisphere you are in. If you're in the Northern Hemisphere, face south; in the Southern Hemisphere, face north. If you are without a compass, look at the ecliptic (i.e., the line the sun follows as it moves through the sky). The sun always rises in the east and sets in the west. Once you decide where the sun has risen, you can figure out where south (Northern Hemisphere) or north (Southern Hemisphere) is, and face that way. If you are facing south, west is to your right and east is to your left. If you find yourself reading this in confusion, don't worry; you'll figure it out.

NEXT STEPS

Now, if the sun is in the middle of the sky as you face south or north, it's noon—12:00 p.m. However, it's possible local time is not following this, due to daylight saving

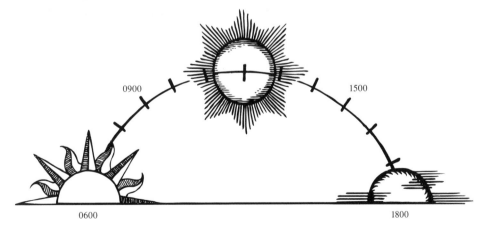

rules; you may find that it is officially 1:30 p.m. local time. (If there's a bear, you can ask him.)

If the sun is not in the exact center, you will have to do more figuring. You can use imaginary sectors to divide the sky into hours, and find the approximate time.

SECTORS IN THE SKY

Estimate the number of hours between sunrise and sunset. If you don't have an idea of the time of sunrise and sunset, you can do your best with a guesstimate. A winter day can be roughly 10 hours long, while a summer day can be 14 hours long. Spring and autumn days tend to be about 12 hours long—closest to 12 hours if you know it to be late March or early September (the equinoxes). You should use these approximate timings based on what you know.

Now, divide the sun's path: look at its arc and visualize sectors. Each of these should equal the number of hours in the day (e.g., six in the eastern half, six in the western half of the ecliptic during spring or autumn). Use your fists to count the sky into sectors if you have trouble visualizing the sectors.

ARITHMETIC NEEDED

You may find that your fist doesn't count for exactly an hour. Let's say you have nine fists in the eastern half, nine in the western—18 fists from sunrise to sunset. It's probably easier to use minutes instead of hours. OK, half a day is six hours, that's 360 minutes. Divide 360 by nine and you get 40. One fist is 40 minutes.

GET BUSY WITH YOUR FISTS

Count the number of fists that the sun has traveled, and this will tell you how many daytime hours have passed. If you know the time of sunrise or sunset, you can then figure out the approximate time. If you don't, you'll have to guess how many hours of daylight there are. If you are confident there are approximately 12 hours of daylight, you can do your best to work through the ecliptic with your fists, and predict how long you have before sunset.

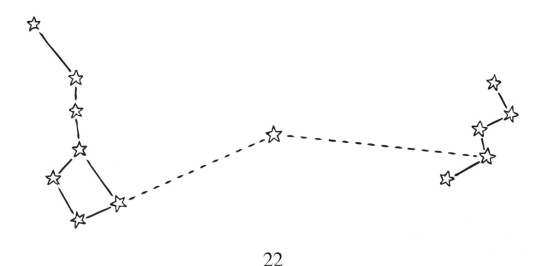

22
GET YOUR BEARINGS FROM THE MOON AND STARS

NAVIGATE AT NIGHT

On a clear night with a visible moon and stars, you are guaranteed to find your way and navigate safely with just a little knowledge. Sailors have developed the technique of celestial navigation over thousands of years, long before the invention of satellite technology.

THE MOON

As with navigation by the sun, this is more a way of pointing you in roughly the right direction. The moon rises in the east and sets in the west. If the moon appears *before* sunset, then its illuminated side is west and it shows where west is. If the moon only appears *after* sunset, it will show where east is. This is only roughly accurate. It is subject to errors depending on your latitude, the season, and the inclination of the moon's orbit. The moon's orbit varies by as much as 10 degrees over several years.

On a clear night with a full moon, you can get your bearings with the help of a stick hammered into flat ground. Mark with stones the two occasions when the shadow is at its longest. You can also mark the end of the shadow at four 20-minute intervals. The line drawn between the first stone and the last stone will provide you with an east-west line. Lay a stick or stones to mark this line. The top of the line, where the first stone was laid, points east. The opposite end points west. When the sun comes up, find a clear landmark, such as a mountain, or large, distant tree, to keep your bearings, as this compass is not portable.

THE STARS

No seasonal corrections are needed when navigating by the stars, but which stars you see does depend on where you are on the globe and will vary for the northern and southern latitudes. There are several clearly visible star formations that can give you accurate indications of direction, both in the Southern Hemisphere and in the Northern. Here is a description of finding north or south from the stars.

In the *Northern Hemisphere*, locate the Big Dipper. Simply use the two stars that make up the edge farthest away from its handle, sometimes called the "pointing stars." These two, lined up, point from the opening of the Big Dipper to the North Star. Count five lengths of the distance between the two "pointing stars," and you'll find the North Star.

The North Star (Polar Star) is found between the Big Dipper and Cassiopeia.

In the *Southern Hemisphere*, you need to find the Southern Cross constellation. Then, draw an imaginary line along the long axis of the Southern Cross four and half times the length of the axis, then follow this imaginary line to earth. This is south. Take note of a landmark in that area or drive a stick diagonally into the ground to show where your line has dropped to earth. This way you will still know where south is in the morning.

If you are unsure of your constellations, you can still use the stars to find out rough directions. Simply find a star you like and mark its position relative to hills or trees or your own position. Now, sit and wait. In the Northern Hemisphere, if the star seems to fall as time goes by, you are facing west. If the star curves flatly to the left, you are facing east. In the Southern Hemisphere, simply reverse these rules.

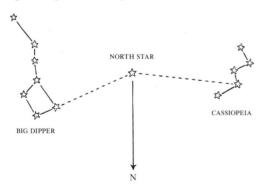

Fig. 1—Finding the North Star

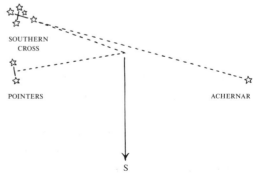

Fig. 2—Using the Southern Cross to find south

BOOK THREE

LAND WILDERNESS

23
LIFE IN THE WILD

The wilderness may be devoid of electricity, roads, and houses, but it is very highly populated. Observing life in the wild may be the motivation for your excursion. Dangerous animals do not pose as much of a challenge to your survival and safety as the rest of the environment. You should, however, employ care and common sense to avoid unpleasant or deadly encounters with your fellow residents of the great outdoors.

AVOID LARGE ANIMALS

It should be relatively simple to avoid very large animals. Bears should always be avoided. If you are in an area populated by bears, look out for bear droppings and recent bear tracks. If you do spot signs of bears, start to walk away in the opposite direction, talking loudly, to alert any nearby bears of your proximity and to avoid a surprise meeting.

Alligators of any large size, especially those longer than nine feet (three meters), should be given a wide berth. Never approach or feed an alligator, as attacks often follow such feedings. If you do find yourself face-to-face with a crocodile or an alligator, back away, but be sure that in doing so you are not placing yourself between the animal and the nearest water.

Lions or any large cats should not be approached. At the first sign that one is near you, leave. If it is close and you think it may attack, open your shirt to make yourself look bigger and make loud noises. If it springs at you, fight back vigorously while protecting your neck from its bite.

Other large animals with hooves, horns, or antlers should be considered with caution. Never try to pet any wild animal, regardless of its size or seemingly docile nature.

INSECTS AND SPIDERS

More people die each year from allergic reactions to bee stings than succumb to shark or alligator attacks. It is wise to look for small visitors in your camp, in your shoe, or dangling from branches.

Watch out for scorpions, which reside in deserts, jungles, and other warm areas of the world. They give a nasty sting, but it is rarely fatal except to small children, the elderly, or the infirm. Centipedes and millipedes may bite, and some are poisonous. Any danger will come mostly from infection where their claws puncture your skin. Always brush them from your skin in the direction they are moving and wash any scratches with warm soapy water.

Avoid wasps, bees, and hornets, especially if you have an allergy.

Ticks can be found in tropical and temperate regions and can transmit various diseases, including Lyme disease, Rocky Mountain spotted fever, and encephalitis. A tick must be attached for at least six hours to pass on these diseases, so check your exposed skin regularly and wear insect repellent.

Spiders such as the fiddleback spider of North America will give a nasty bite that may leave you ill for a week. The red widow spider of the Middle East can have a fatal bite. The tarantula is known for its large size and hairiness. It can be red, brown, or black and has a painful bite. This spider can be found in both the desert and the tropics, and one species lives in Europe. Most are not deadly, but the size of their bite may cause bleeding and infection.

The funnel-web spider of Australia is considered deadly, and at the very least the bite will cause severe pain, sweating, shivering, and weakness for a week. Spiders should never be approached, touched, or handled unless you are very sure of the species.

SNAKES

There are many varieties of snakes in most regions of the world. Local knowledge will help identify those that are poisonous. Never go barefoot, and wear long pants to reduce exposed skin near the ground. Snakes will generally remain unseen and will avoid you. Some snakes, such as the mamba of South Africa, the rattlesnake, or the king cobra of South Asia, have been known to attack people without provocation.

To avoid accidentally being bitten, do the following:

- Do not sleep next to trees or tall grass, and use mosquito netting to dissuade snakes from biting you while you sleep.
- Do not stick your hands into dark crevices or hollow logs.
- Watch where you are walking.
- Do not pick up venomous snakes.
- Do not pick up dead snakes; chop off the head first to make sure they cannot bite you.

FISH

Some fish are pretty, and many are tasty to eat. Others will attack you, will inflict painful stings if you touch them, or will poison you if you eat them. When considering eating a fish, avoid any that do not have scales. Fish that live in shallow water around lagoons or reefs should also be avoided, since they are probably bottom-feeders and you will get a stomach full of the garbage they've collected.

Fish and other sea animals that may inflict painful stings should you step on or touch them live in various parts of the world. Zebrafish mostly live in the Pacific and Indian Oceans, are between one and three feet (30 and 100 centimeters) long, and have sharp spines in their fins whose sting is extremely painful and debilitating to a swimmer. Stonefish are about one foot (30 centimeters) long and live in tropical waters. The fins on their backs inflict a sting that may be fatal if you step on one. The blue-ringed octopus of Australia is gray with distinctive blue rings, and will bite if stepped on or handled. It is very poisonous and its bite can be lethal. The Portuguese man o' war is found in groupings in the tropics, but is sometimes carried to Europe or North America by the Gulf Stream. It looks like a jellyfish. Its tentacles can be as long as 36 feet (11 meters), and its sting is very painful but not usually fatal.

SHELLS

The mollusks that inhabit even attractive-looking shells can be dangerous. Cone shells have needlelike teeth that inject venom that causes pain, blindness, paralysis, and sometimes death. They are found in coral reefs and on rocky shorelines in the tropics. The various kinds of terebra or auger shells are similar to cone shells, but can be found in more temperate seas and are not as poisonous.

DO NOT PANIC

Most insects, animals, fish, snakes, and even shells will happily go about their daily lives without wanting to do you harm. Take heart. You are much more likely to succumb to food poisoning, dehydration, heatstroke, hypothermia, or starvation than to die as a result of an attack by unfriendly wildlife.

24
LOCATE AND OBTAIN FRESH WATER

FINDING WATER

Water is essential to survival. When stopping to make camp, locating a fresh water supply is essential. Water is also very heavy, so while it is important to always carry water when hiking, knowing how to find it easily during your expedition may remove some of the stress of overpacking. Go downhill to look for water, as it is usually found in valleys and ravines. A dry riverbed or an area of lush vegetation can be a source of hidden water no matter where you are. Digging in these places can yield water with a little effort. Crevices in mountains with greenery or bird droppings nearby may be an indication of a spring.

FOLLOWING THE TRAIL

Observing wildlife around you can give great clues to finding water. Following a game trail downhill is also a great way to find water. If you are not lucky enough to find such a neat path, check the sky. Small grain-feeding birds need to find water regularly and can be followed or the rough direction of their flight can be ascertained. Bees and hornets build nests within a couple of miles (kilometers) of fresh water. While it is not possible to ask for directions,

spotting bees will at least indicate that some water is nearby and that your search is not hopeless. An abundance of insects is also a good sign of water, as flies usually stay within 100 yards (91 meters) of it.

Barrel cactus

PLANTS

If a stream, river, or pond is proving elusive, do not despair. Rainwater can be harvested from plants. Vines may be cut high and tilted to drain them of water. Once they run dry, repeat by cutting higher. Bamboo may be tapped low down with a knife and the trapped rainwater harvested.

Fresh rainwater that is collected in clean containers and not left to stand is safe to drink. In arid regions, cacti are a great source of water. Both the barrel cactus of North and South America and the prickly pear are good water containers. Simply cut the plant, then smash the pulp and strain it to retrieve the water.

SNOW

Snow may be boiled to melt it into drinkable water; however, ice yields twice as much with half the fuel. If you are using ice that is near or on the sea, pick the bluest ice you can find. This will indicate its age—the older, the better. White ice near the sea will be laden with salt and is unpleasant to drink. Even blue ice that has been sprayed by the sea may prove too salty to drink without distilling.

DEW AND CONDENSATION

If no water-laden plants, rivers, or ice are at hand, do not wring your hands in despair. Tie a plastic bag over a branch without pressing on the leaves. Leave it in place for a few hours or overnight and then retrieve the water. It will not be a great quantity of liquid, so you may need to set out bags on several branches.

If you are thirsty and walking through rain-soaked foliage, tie clean pieces of cloth on your ankles. When they are soaked, squeeze them out and drink up.

OTHER SOURCES

There are still other methods of hydrating yourself that may not be quite as pleasant as sucking on rain-soaked clothing. Fish eyes contain fresh water and may be sucked, as can fish spines, although not shark spines. Salt water, water from your car, and even urine and blood (preferably animal blood) is safe to drink once it is distilled. There are a number of sources that should always be avoided. Never drink ink, other hazardous liquids, or any water from a pond that looks stagnant or has animal bones next to it. Drinking salt water can cause kidney failure if you do not have enough fresh water to rid your body of the excess sodium.

NO WATER

If you have no way of getting more water than what you have, close your mouth, stop talking or moving unnecessarily, and seriously consider cutting short your excursion.

25
PURIFY WATER

THE EASY WAY

Your trusty survival kit, which you packed with such care before departing, will, among its many treasures, include water sterilization tablets. In this case, follow the instructions on the packet carefully and enjoy the resulting safe, clean drinking water. If you failed to pack these tablets, there is another way. Indeed, you may consider that packing such an item in your survival pack is not truly adventurous.

FIRE

Essential to all good camps, fire adds warmth, color, and a sense of hominess to the wilderness. In addition, it also enables you to cook, scare away insects and predators, and purify water. Boiling water will rid it of 90 percent of known waterborne diseases. All water you retrieve in the wild, unless it is fresh rainwater, should be purified by boiling for 10 minutes, then covered and allowed to cool or used immediately for hot beverages.

NO FIRE

If you find yourself unable to light a fire, due to either inclement weather or the need to continue hiking, you will need to resort to your water sterilization tablets. This may be the moment to review your earlier position on the necessity of this item. If you have very large muscles, you may also choose to carry very large amounts of water, previously boiled, as you hike. Should it be raining as you walk, carry a container to collect rainwater. Simply tie a clean, empty tin can to a large stick. You may even tie a container to your head, if you are very thirsty. Rainwater collection at your campsite will be of great benefit if you have no fire, because it is safe to drink if the container is clean and the water is not left to sit uncovered.

A SOCK AND A BOTTLE

It is possible to remove silt and particles from water using a sock and a plastic bottle. Simply cut the top off a plastic bottle of any size. Take a clean sock and pull it over the bottle to cover the opening. Then, slowly pour water into the bottle. The material of the sock will remove the bits of debris from the water, leaving it clear. If you are not confident of your sock being clean, use any clean material stuffed into the opening of any container. This will not make the water safe to drink, as bacteria might still be present. It will simply remove discoloration and may remove bad odor or taste from the water. You can also use a coffee filter. You should still boil this water to remove any bacteria.

CHLORINE

Adding a few drops of chlorine bleach will make water safe or ensure that bottles and containers are disinfected. The amount of bleach you use will depend on the percentage of chlorine in it. Do not use containers to store water that have been used to store milk or fruit juice. Do not use bleach that is fragranced or has added household cleaning ingredients.

If it is regular bleach, one drop for each cup of water should work. Add the bleach, shake or stir well, and allow the mixture to sit uncovered for 30 minutes. If the water does not smell slightly of bleach, repeat the process. To improve the taste, sprinkle some salt and sugar into the water before drinking. This water may be stored safely— once it is sealed and kept out of the sun— for a number of weeks. If you are using a water bottle, open the lid slightly and shake it to allow the bleached water to splash on the inside of the lid and the threads on the top. This will stop any bacteria that are on the threads from reinfecting the water when you drink it later. Close the bottle tightly.

26
SELECT FOOD YOU CAN EAT

EATING IN THE WILD

Part of the joy of spending time in the great outdoors is the experience of finding your own food. A word of caution, however: it is best to be fully equipped with all of the food you may need to keep you nourished for the duration of your trip. It is better if hunting and foraging are enjoyable, leisurely pursuits rather than motivated by potential starvation or to fend off cannibalistic tendencies among your party.

TYPES OF FOOD

What types of food you can forage and eat in the wild will vary depending on where you are and what season it is. By the seaside, you may find yourself harvesting seaweed, mollusks, sea cucumbers, and limpets. You may also fish and try to hunt seabirds.

In a forest, small mammals may be hunted, and plants, mushrooms, and nuts may be found. Birds, eggs, and insects can also be caught or collected for your dinner.

In tropical areas, there is a vast array of fruits that are edible. Reptiles or birds can also be hunted, as can small mammals. Insects are abundant and varied and will find you whether you want to find them or not.

In arctic climates, plant life is limited, and hunting and fishing will be more likely to yield dinner.

Take time before your trip to research possible wild food in the area to which you wish to travel. Take guidebooks to help you identify safe plants and fish, or palatable mammals and birds, before you commence foraging or hunting. There are poisonous plants and animals in all parts of the world.

CHECKING FOOD

A good guidebook with color illustrations of plants that are safe and those that are poisonous is very helpful. It should list characteristics of the leaf, flower, stem, and berries of the plant. Some plants look quite different when they are in blossom. If the roots are unusual, they may also help you identify a plant.

Never eat a plant that looks withered, or one that has been trampled or is covered in fungus or insects. Always choose a plant that you have confidently identified and that is clean and healthy-looking.

Similar guides to birds, fish, shellfish, and small mammals should also be considered essential if you plan to forage and hunt while you travel.

If you cannot easily identify a plant or, having consulted your fellow travelers and your guidebook, are unsure, it is probably best to move on and avoid eating it. Mushrooms, unless you are experienced in picking them, should be avoided unless you are using a reliable guidebook. Many safe mushrooms are easily confused with very poisonous ones. Toxic mushrooms do not taste unpleasant, nor are they rendered safe with cooking. Insects may feed safely on them, but this should not be considered an indication that they are edible for human beings.

TESTING PLANTS

If you are determined to try out an unknown plant, proceed with caution. First, take a fresh-looking piece of the plant and crush it to ensure that it does not smell like bitter almonds or peaches, as this may indicate poison. Then, rub the juice of the crushed piece on your skin. If a rash, swelling, or itching occurs, wash the area thoroughly and do not add this plant to your menu.

If your skin is happy, take a small piece of the plant, put it on your lips, and count to 20. Should nothing unpleasant occur, place a small amount on your tongue and again count to 20, or get your friend to count for you. If no swelling, burning, itching, or soreness occurs, place the piece inside your mouth under your tongue and wait for about 20 seconds. Should you still feel well and brave, commence chewing, and, should this not make you pause, swallow the piece of plant.

You are indeed an intrepid outdoor adventurer. Now you need to wait for five hours without ingesting any other food or drink. All other members of your party not taking part in the test may freely eat and drink from your safe camp food supplies. If at any time you experience pain, excessive gas, nausea, vomiting, or abdominal swelling, try to induce yourself to vomit, drink hot water, and, should symptoms persist, seek medical attention quickly.

27

FORAGE IN WOODLAND AND JUNGLE TERRAIN

EAT ALMOST ANYTHING

The key to any healthy diet is to vary your food and ensure you get a good amount of fats, carbohydrates, and proteins, not forgetting vitamins and minerals. Be open-minded about your foraging. Do not shirk from things simply because you would not serve them at your dinner table at home. Once you are sure the item is not poisonous or inedible, by all means consider it, regardless of how slimy it is, how many legs it has, or how long you need to chew it.

PLANTS IN THE WOODS

All woodlands and jungles contain edible plants. Having a description and picture of one or two seasonal plants in the area will ensure that you will have greens on your plate. White berries and any plant with milky sap should always be avoided. In Northern Hemisphere woodlands in the autumn, you may find berries, such as blackberries, thimbleberries, Juneberries, or salmonberries. These can be eaten straight from the plant. You can make tea from the leaves of salmonberries. Nettle leaves may be picked, cooked, and eaten like spinach or used for tea. Cow parsnip flower stems whose flowers are unopened can be peeled and cooked as a vegetable. You can even have a nice coffee substitute if you find some wild chicory by drying and grinding down its roots. If you are less choosy or starving, try some pine needles or the inside of beech bark, which can be chewed raw.

INSECTS

Plant life provides a good source of vitamins. And green vegetables such as nettles provide you with carbohydrates. For much-needed protein and fat, should trapping and hunting prove unsuccessful or too time-consuming, insects should be on your menu. They are nutritious, easy to find and catch, and may have a very interesting texture, especially when eaten raw and wriggling.

Move rotten wood in order to uncover beetle larvae. Grubs and caterpillars can also provide a tasty snack or an addition to your salad. Crickets, grasshoppers, and locusts can be eaten raw once you pinch their heads off. Snails and worms can be cooked and added to soups.

IN THE JUNGLE

Peel all fruits you find once you have safely identified them, as the peel may contain bacteria that will make you ill. When in the jungle, only eat what you can peel or cook. Avoiding all brightly colored insects and those that sting is a good rule for safe

Wild chicory

foraging. You may find bananas, mangoes, or other fruit usually found in the supermarket. Remember that the climate in the jungle will make food spoil quickly. Once it is peeled, cooked, or beheaded, eat it immediately.

EGGS

For a full and satisfying breakfast, find a convenient nest in a tree, in a bush, or on the ground and retrieve the eggs. These may be fried, boiled, or baked. The parents may object to your theft, so prepare to retreat hastily.

WHAT TO AVOID

Do not eat spiders in any part of the world, or any insect or other animal that feeds on blood, such as mosquitoes or leeches. Do not eat any fish with bristles or spines rather than scales. Most insects can be eaten raw, apart from the head, while some snails and worms need to be cooked, so to be sure to cook anything without legs. Do not attempt to eat wasps, as they can sting even when they are dead. Wasp larvae may be eaten, but foraging for wasp larvae may be risky.

28

FORAGE IN HARD TERRAIN: POLAR REGIONS, DESERTS, AND MOUNTAINS

GREENERY

Regardless of whether you are in a polar region, in the desert, or high in the mountains, keep a lookout for the color green. This is where you may find plant life to eat, as well as insects or other mammals to hunt, and thus stave off your hunger pains.

IN A POLAR CLIMATE

It is unlikely that plant life will be available to you here. Seals, fish, and penguins may be the best source of food.

Seals should be approached from behind and only hunted when they are out of the sea. Penguins should be approached with caution, being careful to avoid their flippers, which are surprisingly strong. Fishing nets, hooks, a harpoon or spear, or even a club may be used to catch your meal. It may be possible to hunt arctic birds, hares, and foxes. In the autumn, large herds of caribou, which are like deer, migrate south and may be hunted. It is best to avoid polar bears, as they are very dangerous and large and will attack humans.

IN A DESERT

There are not many things to eat in a desert. It is important to remember that if you are very thirsty, eating will make you thirstier, so avoid food.

There are some plants found in the desert that are edible. The fruit of the date palm, if found when the fruit is ripe, can be very tasty. It is bitter when unripe. Flowering plants such as the acacia would be a great find; their flowers, pods, and leaves can all be eaten raw. Others, such as the agave, have flowers and flower buds that are edible once cooked. Cacti are possibly your most likely find, and many types are edible. With the exception of the barrel cactus, which is safe, avoid any with a milky sap.

Reptiles can be a great source of protein when in the desert and may not be hard to catch, especially at the start of the day. All reptiles carry salmonella on their skin so they need to be well cooked. Wash your hands carefully after preparing your snake or other reptile for cooking to avoid nasty stomach cramps and vomiting.

IN THE MOUNTAINS

At high altitude, animals and plant life are naturally scarcer. You may have to consider eating pine needles or beech bark.

Mushrooms will provide a tastier

meal. Not all mushrooms are safe; some are deadly. Ensure that you study them carefully. Even experienced mushroom gatherers have mistakenly eaten poisonous species. Most mushroom-related deaths are still attributed to young children foraging near their homes. If you are unsure, avoid mushrooms.

Mountain ash, a tree that favors higher altitudes of up to 6,000 feet (2,000 meters), is also known as the rowan tree. The fruits of this tree, which are bright red berries, appear in autumn and can be eaten raw, although they are quite bitter. These berries provide more vitamin C than lemons. They can be pressed for juice or even turned into jam. They also attract birds, which may provide an additional source of food.

Birds and bird eggs may be found and cooked. Look in bushes, cracks in rocks, and in trees to find nests. Do not be tempted to scale sheer rock for your cooked breakfast unless you are an experienced climber and have ropes. Birds may attack you if they perceive you are a threat to their nests, and they may make your descent to safety difficult.

Once again, insects may be abundant at higher altitudes regardless of the season and may provide a much-needed snack on your hike.

29
BUILD A GOOD SHELTER

LOCATION, LOCATION, LOCATION

Pick a sheltered area with flat, dry ground, near but not next to water. Being too close to water will attract a lot of insects, and the area could also flood. Areas to avoid include hilltops, which will be exposed; ravines, which will be damp; solitary trees, which may attract lightning; and dry riverbeds, which may turn into rivers if it rains. If you are trying to attract attention, or wish to be rescued, reconsider the hilltop.

QUICK SHELTER

The purpose of a shelter is to keep you safe, warm, and dry. The smaller the shelter, the quicker it is to make and the easier it is to heat. If you are short on materials, time, or companions, or are just short, consider turning your poncho into a lean-to. First, find two conveniently placed trees about eight feet (two and a half meters) apart. Take two pieces of rope, each about three feet (one meter) long. Fold away the hood of the poncho, and use your ropes to stretch the poncho between the trees at waist height. Stretch the other side of the poncho to the ground and secure it to the ground with small stakes.

To avoid getting wet and cold, make sure the back of your shelter acts as a windbreak. Lay dry leaves, pine needles, or any similar material you have on the ground to help keep you warm. If you do not want to sit up, tie a long rope between the two trees at knee height and drape the poncho over the rope, securing it to the ground on both sides. Prepare the ground as before, and crawl in.

NO MATERIALS

If you are without a tent, poncho, waterproof sheet, parachute, or knife and want to make a shelter, it is still possible. First, find a tree that has partially fallen over, or find some large branches that have recently broken off of a tree. Tie the branch to a nearby tree at waist height to make a lean-to. Lay other fallen branches and leaves against your lean-to and fill in any gaps. Layer the ground with leaves and make a nice fire near the opening. If you are using a partially felled tree, make sure it does not intend to continue falling to the ground in the near future (and therefore onto you).

TROPICAL SHELTER

Staying off of the ground and dry is your main concern in a tropical climate. Bamboo is a fantastic building material and grows in many places in the world. Carefully cut four long pieces and secure them into the ground in a rectangle. Cut two of them a little shorter so that your roof will be sloped. Cut more bamboo, split horizontally, and flatten for roof tiles, saving one unflattened piece to use as a gutter. Make a frame for the roof. Lay the bamboo on the roof frame so that the cut side of every second one faces down so they will interlock like roof tiles. Lash them to the frame at the ends.

Alternatively, make a frame and lay extra sticks across it. Then, using large leaves or palms, interlace them to make your roof. This roof may leak a little.

Keeping off of the ground will help keep you dry and away from some of the insect life. Make a bed using bamboo or other convenient wood. Drive the four legs into the ground, allowing a comfortable length for lying down. Then, cut two shorter pieces for the ends and additional short pieces for the bed base. Lay large leaves on top until you achieve a mattresslike effect.

SNOWY TERRAIN

Should attempting to build an igloo prove beyond your time constraints or skill set, there are alternatives. Look around for a tree that is partially submerged by snow. Lower branches may be lifted up to reveal a hollow. Compress the snow on the sides of the hollow, lay leaves on the floor, and climb in.

If there are no trees around, you will need to dig a trench at least as long as you are tall and about two feet (60 centimeters) deep. Then, cut about 10 snow bricks. Lay the bricks over the trench on either side so that they meet in a peaked roof. Fill any gaps with loose snow. Close up one end, leaving the other open end as a door and for air. Lay whatever material you have on the floor as insulation. Then you are free to climb down into your coffinlike bed for a good night's sleep.

HEAD IN THE SAND?

If you are on sandy terrain and need to build a shelter, start by looking around for any driftwood or debris you can use as supports and for digging. Dig a tunnel so that the opening faces away from the sun, as this will keep it cooler. It needs to be both long enough and wide enough to lie down in. Lay driftwood across the top of the shelter and mound soil or sand on top. You can then widen the entrance and place whatever you can find down on the floor to make it more comfortable.

OTHER IDEAS

Is there a cave nearby without any large predators in residence? Check it carefully. Scare any small residents away by lighting a small fire at the back of the cave, as this will smoke them out. Fashion a door using rocks, logs, or branches. Security may be an issue, as inclement weather may induce animals to make for your newly acquired property for shelter.

Do you have a parachute that you don't need? Open it up and hang it from a high tree branch to create a tepee. Make a rip to create a door, and stake the parachute to the ground. A more elaborate tepee may be constructed by lashing three long poles together securely at the top. Place them upright, then pull out the lower ends and tie them to the ground. Any waterproof material, even pine branches, may be layered around or draped over this basic structure. Ensure that there is adequate ventilation. If you have more people to house, use six longer poles.

30
MAKE TOOLS

If you are feeling creative or are in desperate need of weapons or tools while in the wild, you can easily fashion some using stone or bone, following the example of your prehistoric forebears.

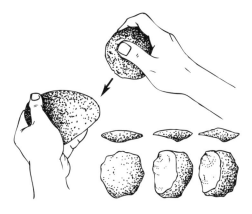

Making stone chips

STONE TOOLS

For the strongest stone tools, use obsidian, which is a black volcanic rock found in many places in the world. It has a naturally sharp edge and is used to manufacture surgical tools. Simply using a hammer or round stone, hit the piece of obsidian to make pieces flake away. These shards will be sharp. It is best to place material in your hand around a stone flake before using it for cutting, so that you are not the thing that ends up sliced. If no obsidian is handy, chert or quartzite rock is the next best thing.

You can also find a strong-looking pebble, slightly bigger than your fist. Smash it in half to create a flat surface and then break off the top to create another flat edge. Take your pebble and, striking at an angle, chip away at the other three edges. Once

this is done, strike downward on the top flat edge to flake off a sliver of rock. This can be used as an arrowhead, spearhead, or knife, depending on the size. You may make more than one blade from each pebble. Simply chip the edges again and then flake off another shard. Flint may be used as a cutting tool. Hit a larger piece of flint with a stone and flake off shards.

BONE TOOLS

If the terrain means that stone is in short supply, bone can be very easily transformed into useful tools. Shoulder blades can have teeth cut into one side using a knife or stonecutter. One half of a sizable antler

can be used as a spade. Smaller bones can be converted into needles for sewing by simply sharpening one end and gouging a small hole in the other. Animal horns can be used as knives or stakes, with little or no sharpening needed.

OTHER MATERIALS

Sticks of hardwood may be sharpened and burned at one end to create a spear or arrow. A more effective method is to tip the arrow or spear with a knife, a piece of sharp bone, or a sharpened stone you have prepared. Fishhooks can be made from thorns. Pieces of bamboo can be used as crude shovels, cut and sharpened to create weapons, or even used as raw material to fashion cups and bowls for your camp.

Empty tin cans can also be used to fashion tools. Open and flatten out the can and then fold it into a triangular shape. This can be cut to sharpen it further. Pieces of tin are useful as spearheads and arrowheads.

You may wish to attach your newly fashioned bone, stone, or tin knife to a piece of wood. First, select a suitable piece of wood for the purpose. Cut a notch in the top of the wood, slightly smaller than the width of the blade. The depth of the notch will depend on whether you are creating a knife, a spear, or an arrow. A good guide is to make it about one-fifth the length of the blade. Wedge the blade in place. Protect your hands while doing this. Then, bind the blade in place using string, wire, vines, or cloth material torn into strips.

RETRIEVING THE WOOD

If you don't have enough wood lying around near your camp, it may be necessary to chop down a tree. For this, you will need an axe. You can fashion an axe yourself, although in this case you may wish to choose only narrow trees to cut down. Make sure you tie your axe head very securely to the handle to prevent it from flying off at speed.

To use your axe efficiently, remember that repeated blows of medium force directed at an angle of 45 degrees are better than full-force blows aimed straight at your target. Swinging your axe too hard will cause it to jam in the wood. If you try to hit the tree too fast, you risk missing your chosen target or glancing off the wood. This could result in hitting yourself with the axe, which is not what you want. You may also miss hitting the tree with the axe head and hit it with the axe handle, causing the handle to break. This will certainly delay you, as you will then have to find wood to replace your axe handle.

Choose a tree to fell that is not too tall or wide. If there are large trees growing close together, they may stop the fall of your tree. Remove all vines or small branches from the place on the trunk where you plan to chop.

Decide where you wish the tree to fall. If the tree is growing on a slope or has more branches on one side, it will want to fall that way. On the side *opposite* from where you want the tree to fall, make a cut that is less than halfway through the trunk. Then, move to the opposite side and make a similar cut lower down on the tree trunk. The tree should fall on this side. If the tree does not want to budge, make cuts deeper on each side. Make sure you are well clear of the tree once it begins to move. Shout out a warning to those in the vicinity.

With this new raw material of wood, you are ready to defend yourself, make a shelter, dig a toilet, or go hunting.

31
TIE KNOTS THAT WORK

PRACTICE MAKES PERFECT

As with fire making, knot tying is an important technique for any outdoor adventurer to master. It is best to learn and practice some basic knots before embarking. Here are a few that may be useful in varying situations.

REEF KNOT

This is also called a square knot and is useful in first aid. It is a method of joining two ropes of equal thickness and it lies flat. First, imagine you are tying your shoelaces. Pick up an end of each rope, overlap them and bring one end under the other, and pull. Repeat for a double knot. You can make a bow at this point, but it is not traditional. You may wish to secure the ends with a half hitch each if they are too long.

HALF HITCHES

This knot is useful for both tying off the loose ends of rope after securing other knots, and also for securing rope to a ring,

pole, or tree. Take your rope and wrap it around the tree leaving at least one foot (30 centimeters) of rope at the open end for tying. Then, pass the open end of the rope over the length of rope and then through the newly created loop. Repeat this process and pull. This is a useful knot since it is quick and is easily untied.

SHEET BEND

This knot will secure two ropes of unequal thickness. First, take the thicker rope and make a loop with it. Then, take the thinner rope and pass it into the loop, then around behind the loop and back again, passing it once under itself. Pull gently, gradually increasing pressure to make the knot secure and tight. Ensure that equal pressure is placed on this knot to prevent slipping. Check and tighten it regularly if you are unsure.

FISHERMAN'S KNOT

If you are attempting to tie fishing line, soaked gut, or vines, this is the knot for you. Bear in mind that this may prove impossible to untie and is not suitable for bulky rope, where a reef knot should be used instead.

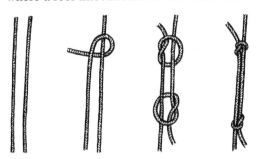

To start, lay the ropes on the ground next to one another with the open ends facing in opposite directions. Ensure that at least one foot (30 centimeters) of each rope is next to the other. Make a loop near the end of rope A by doubling up the end of the rope. Ensure that rope B passes through this loop. Then, run the open end of rope A through the loop and pull loosely. Repeat this process with rope B. The ropes should still be lying flat and next to one another. Gradually ease the two knots so that they meet in the center. Pull until the knot is tight.

BOWLINE

This knot is useful in making a lifeline because the loop you create will not reduce in size even when pulled. This will enable you to pull someone to safety from a ravine or into your boat without accidentally crushing him or her.

First, make a small loop in the rope, allowing a couple of feet (60 centimeters) of rope to hang loose at the end with which you will be working. Take the open end of rope and pass it through the loop, around the main length of rope, and finally back through the loop again. Pull to tighten. To make this more secure, take the short loose end and make a half hitch knot with it and the main length of rope.

SAFETY

For safety, always double-check knots, have others inspect your work, and retighten any knots regularly. For nearly all knots, avoid using nylon rope or line, as it will slip.

32
BE A HUNTER IN THE WILD

GET ARMED

To truly enter the spirit of adventure, try fashioning your own weapons for hunting. The bow and arrow will allow you to kill small- to medium-sized mammals or birds with relatively little practice. A club is an extremely easy weapon to fashion. You may simply wish to rename a suitable piece of wood. This can be handy for killing snakes or reptiles or dealing with injured animals you have trapped. A spear can be used for both throwing and stabbing, and is also easy to make.

CHOOSE WOOD FOR YOUR BOW

Dry but not cracked hardwood is needed to make a bow. Oak, hickory, yew, or teak are all suitable. The piece should be three feet (one meter) long and have no limbs, knots, or twists in it. Take your time to find the best piece of wood for your bow. Next, bend the stick to see which way it naturally wishes to curve. Shape the bow so that the center of the stick is thicker than the ends and create a notch on each end to hold the string. The notch should be cut one to two inches (two to five centimeters) from the ends of the bow.

STRING

There are many materials you can use for your bowstring, including twine, vines, animal sinew, fishing line, or nylon rope. It is important that the string is taut and does not stretch out longer when you pull back on the bow.

ARROWS

Find as many very straight sticks as you can. They should be half the length of the finished bow. Cut to size and then, using your knife, whittle them until they are smooth. If they are not completely straight, warm them over a fire and then hold them straight as they cool. Then, cut a small notch at the end so that the arrow will stay on the string.

ARROWHEADS

If you lack suitable materials, simply carve the point of the arrow and heat it over a fire to harden it. It is better to attach arrowheads. These can be made from bone, stone shards, metal from used tin cans, or pieces of glass. Cut a notch at the top of the arrow shaft, fit the chosen arrowhead, and lash it with whatever string, cord, or other material you have available.

FLETCHING

Adding feathers to your arrows will improve their flight and accuracy. Attach them to the arrows with glue or make grooves on the arrow shaft and slide the feathers on in this way, securing them with thin thread.

If this sounds like too much hassle, skip this part entirely and proceed with your new weapon to the nearest prey you can spot and start hunting.

33
OBSERVE AND HUNT PREY

TIME OF DAY

Hunting is best done first thing in the morning, so set your alarm clock for dawn. Most animals have better night vision, hearing, and sense of smell than you, so daylight is your friend. For this reason, and to avoid bumping into unseen predators, you should cease hunting in the afternoon.

OBSERVING PREY

In order to stalk prey, you must first locate them. Signs to look for include chewed bark, shrubbery, half-chewed fruit or nuts, signs of soil being dug, or animal bones on the ground. You should also take note of any animal droppings. If they are fresh, they will still be wet and will attract flies. Larger piles will indicate larger animals. Inspecting dung further may indicate what type of food the animal eats.

Probably the best way to determine what prey you are following is its tracks. Tracks are easier to spot on damp ground, snow, or wet sand. If a track has a clear, distinct shape, it is more recent. Small mammal tracks may be very hard to spot unless the ground is very soft.

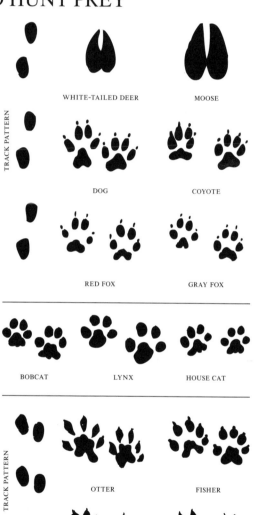

TRACK PATTERN

WHITE-TAILED DEER   MOOSE

DOG   COYOTE

RED FOX   GRAY FOX

BOBCAT   LYNX   HOUSE CAT

TRACK PATTERN

OTTER   FISHER

MINK   WEASEL

TRACK PATTERN

RACCOON

STRIPED SKUNK

PORCUPINE

BEAVER

BLACK BEAR

OPOSSUM

WOODCHUCK

MUSKRAT

TRACK PATTERN

SNOWSHOE HARE

COTTONTAIL RABBIT

GRAY SQUIRREL

WHITE-FOOTED MOUSE

CROW

TURKEY

GOOSE

TIPS ON HUNTING

When stalking prey, remain downwind. Walk slowly and quietly. Test each step with your toe gently to ensure you are not stepping on dry leaves or twigs, then place your foot down heelfirst and test the next step. If you are spotted by your prey, freeze and wait. Many animals do not see stationary objects well. If you have injured an animal and it is not running away, do not approach it. Wait for five or 10 minutes. The animal is then less likely to run or to attack you.

SAFETY

Hunting may lead to dangerous confrontations with animals. Never corner an injured animal, as even a small mammal can bite or scratch, which can lead to infection. If you come face-to-face with a dangerous animal, remain calm. Talk and back away; avoid acting like prey, but do not stare at it. If an animal charges at you, you may simply be blocking its preferred escape route. Try simply moving out of the way. If your urge to run is overwhelming, run in a zigzag pattern, as some animals only charge in straight lines. Drop any supplies or loose clothing as you flee, as this may cause the animal to pause. If you cannot outrun the animal, you may wish to climb a tree. Some predators are very determined and will wait by the tree, so prepare to make yourself comfortable.

Do not attempt to run from wild cats, wild dogs, or bears, as they will treat you as prey and will most certainly outrun you.

ANIMALS TO HUNT

Some animals are very difficult to stalk and trapping them is the better option. All wild cats and dogs have excellent senses and will be almost impossible to stalk. Deer and antelope can be found in nearly all wooded areas of the world. They can be difficult to find and need to be tracked at a distance so they don't startle and run. Wild sheep and goats live in small groups and are shy around humans. It is unwise to chase wild goats on rocky terrain, as they are very likely to escape while you risk injury from falling. If you are in Australia, wild kangaroos can provide edible meat. They are most active at night and you should remain clear of their rear legs to avoid being kicked.

Smaller mammals like squirrels, rabbits, monkeys, wild pigs, possums, raccoons, and rodents may be easier to trap than hunt. Beware of bites and scratches when handling injured animals.

Alligators and crocodiles are hard to spot. It is safest to assume they are there if you are in a known habitat. If they are more than nine feet (three meters) long, hunting them is too dangerous. Smaller ones can be caught on a baited line and then clubbed between the eyes. Their tails are edible.

Lizards that are not poisonous can be caught by the tail, while snakes can be caught using a forked stick and then clubbed. Never try to retrieve your felled snake unless you are sure it is dead. It is safest to chop off its head before picking it up.

A tortoise is slow and easy to catch. Extract and stab or club the head. A tortoise may be cooked by laying it whole in the embers of a fire until its shell cracks.

34
SET A TRAP FOR PREY

Traps are an essential part of most survival strategies. Setting up a few well-positioned traps can save you energy in potentially fruitless hunting expeditions. It is best to set up your trapline at a bit of a distance from your main camp. When you are fit and healthy, you will enjoy the walk, and should you become sick or injured, you will still have potential game to prey on in the immediate vicinity of your camp. Check the traps regularly to prevent your animal from escaping, suffering needlessly, or being taken by other predators.

TYPES OF TRAPS

There are many types of traps, and the type you should use depends on your level of skill, the size of animal you wish to trap, and the materials you have at hand. Large deadfall traps are necessary to fell large mammals, but they may be dangerous to set or may go off accidentally with deadly consequences. A basic snare, a springing snare, and a small deadfall will be useful in trapping many small animals.

CHOOSE YOUR SITE

It is best to establish a well-used animal trail and set your trapline with a variety of well-spaced traps. Places where the forest begins to thin out or obvious approaches to water may be good places for traps. To avoid accidents, ensure that everyone in your group knows the location of all the traps. Check and reset traps. If they remain untried, consider changing the bait or the location. Because animals are more wary when they are close to home, do not place traps too close to their lairs.

Try to camouflage the trap to blend in with the surroundings. Handle the trap as little as possible or wear gloves. If you have no gloves, coat your hands in mud and rotting vegetation found in the area. Avoid stepping on the game trail or your trapline, as this may scare off your prey. Construct your traps well to ensure they will hold the animal and to enable them to be used more than once, thereby saving you work. Construct your traps away from the trapline, and then once they are made, put them in place. You do not want to disturb the area too much, as this may alert your prey.

BAIT

The bait you choose will depend on the animal you seek to trap. Once you have scouted the area and noticed the animal

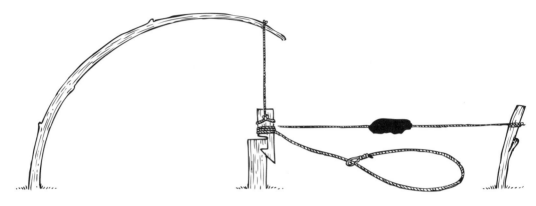

Spring or twitch-up snare

tracks or perhaps spotted potential prey, you need to take note of its food source. If the intended prey eats particular plants, take note of the type and harvest fresh leaves, berries, or fruit from higher in the plant than the animals normally reach and place these in your trap. The most frequently eaten plant will be the favorite. It is best if it is in short supply, as it will be more tempting. Most herbivores will be attracted to cooked grain that is ground and pounded down into a doughlike substance. Peanut butter or salt will also make good bait for small mammals. Scatter some around the trap so that the animal can taste the food first.

SNARE

A simple snare made of string, corded rope, or wire can be successful if placed along a well-used game trail at the correct height. Take a length of wire and twist the end to create a small eyelet. Then, make a loop, threading the length through the eyelet. Make the loop the size of your fist. Suspend the loop from a nearby stake about a hand's length away so that it hovers about a hand's width from the ground. Use twigs found nearby to keep it off the ground if necessary. This will trap small mammals around the neck and larger ones around the leg. Placing suitable bait nearby will attract them to the area.

SPRING OR TWITCH-UP SNARE

First, find a springy sapling at least three feet (one meter) in height. Tie the top with string and bend it over by pulling on the string. Tie a loop to the end of the string and secure this to a notch cut into a stake near the sapling. Test this: if the string is banged, it should break free of the stake and the sapling should spring upright. Next, run a second piece of string from the first and connect it to the loop of a simple snare. This springing snare is good for catching rabbits, which may otherwise break free of a simple snare. To bait your snare, run a second piece of string from the spring trap and secure this to a second stake so that it is stretched above the snare on the ground. Fix the bait onto this stretched string. An animal taking the bait should trigger the spring trap.

DEADFALL TRAP

The larger, heavier, and higher the deadfall trap, the deadlier it will be. To construct a relatively simple and small deadfall trap, take three sticks, one of which should be forked, and sharpen all three upper ends. Drive one stick into the ground securely. Hold the forked stick parallel to the first stick and balance the third on top so that all three remain in place. It may be necessary to place a flat piece of wood under the forked stick so that it balances on the ground. Then, find some heavy logs of the correct height and lean them against the top stick, creating a small lean-to structure. Attach the bait to the forked stick so that it is held under the leaning logs. Any animal that attempts to eat or remove the bait will cause the forked stick to fall. This will result in the heavy logs dropping on the animal. Sharpened stakes can be fixed under the suspended weight of the logs to ensure that a killing blow is delivered.

BE SAFE

Always make sure to remove all traps before leaving an area. Never set up dangerous deadfall traps where others may be hiking or hunting. When testing traps, use a stick or rock. Avoid placing your own body parts into a trap.

35
KILL AND COOK A RABBIT

HOW TO KILL A RABBIT

More than half of the world's rabbits reside in North America. Wild rabbits are also commonly found in Europe. Rabbits are a domesticated animal bred for their meat and fur, but they also make good family pets. If you are attached to your pet rabbit, you may wish to skip this chapter.

You can kill a rabbit quickly and easily by hitting it hard with a club or other solid, heavy implement on the back of the neck. Alternatively, you can also kill a rabbit by holding its back feet and pulling its head firmly down and out (as shown in Fig. 1) to break its neck.

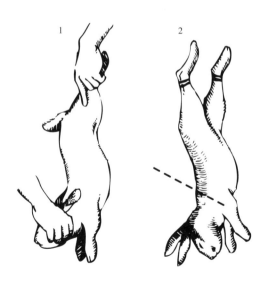

Fig. 1 and 2—How to kill a rabbit

When the rabbit is dead, tie it up by the back feet, cut off its head and front feet, and let the blood drain out (as shown in Fig. 2).

HOW TO SKIN AND CLEAN A RABBIT

Lay the rabbit on a heavy chopping board or block of wood and, with a meat cleaver or old knife and hammer, chop off all the feet just above the knees. Cut off the tail and then, using the same tools and technique, remove the head.

Lift the fur at the belly, make a horizontal incision, and pull the skin away from the rabbit. Insert the knife into the horizontal cut, taking care not to pierce the stomach, and then, holding the knife upside down so the sharp edge faces upward, slowly cut the skin from the belly up to the neck.

Gradually pull the skin away from the rabbit's flesh; if it is fresh, the skin should come away easily. Work your way around the body of the rabbit first and then upward to the front legs. The legs must be popped out through the skin. The best way to do this is to pull out the skin around the leg and push on the stump of the rabbit's leg from the other side—a bit like taking off a jacket.

The final stage is to grip the shoulders of the rabbit and pull the skin down over the back legs—again like removing an item of clothing.

Next, you must paunch or gut the rabbit; this will prevent the meat from spoiling. Make another horizontal cut across the flesh of the belly (try not to pierce the intestines), and gradually slice open the stomach. Reach in and upward to the ribs, grasp the intestines, and remove with one firm tug. Put aside the rabbit's liver for eating—this is the best part!

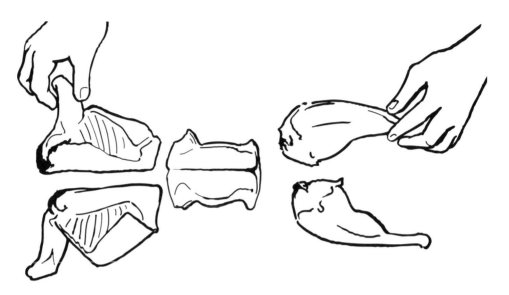

Cut through the diaphragm and pull out the lungs and heart. With a knife, cut out the rabbit's bottom, make two cuts to form a V-shape where the tail was, and remove any remaining droppings from the rectum. Give the rabbit a scrub under running water; it is now ready to be jointed or cooked.

HOW TO JOINT A RABBIT

A rabbit is usually jointed into five sections: the two hind legs, the saddle (the middle part), and the two front legs with some ribcage each. The first chop is made just above the hind legs. Once separated, chop down the middle of the hind legs. Then, chop the top of the saddle just below the ribcage, and split the front legs and torso down the middle.

HOW TO COOK A RABBIT

How you cook your rabbit depends on its age. Younger rabbits are good for roasting and frying and older specimens for stewing. Rabbit meat is very lean and becomes dry very quickly. Stewing always gives the most succulent results. The following recipe is for rabbit and white wine stew, but most of the ingredients can be substituted or even left out. For example, white wine could be red wine, or stock, or water. Onion gives flavor and body, but you can do without the celery or carrot if you do not have it. You can use leek or shallot or more garlic if you have no onion. Tomatoes work, but the stew is fine without them. Rabbit, water, vegetables, and salt stewed for an hour or so will be filling and tasty.

RECIPE: RABBIT AND WHITE WINE STEW

- One rabbit, jointed
- One onion, diced
- One stick celery, diced
- One large carrot, diced
- Three large potatoes, cut into large pieces
- One bottle white wine
- Three cloves garlic, mashed
- Five medium tomatoes, peeled and chopped
- Salt and pepper
- Four tablespoons (60 milliliters) olive oil
- Thyme

Heat the oil in a heavy-bottomed pan or metal casserole dish, preferably one large enough to brown your jointed rabbit in one go. Brown the pieces of rabbit on both sides for a few minutes. Remove. Soften the onion, celery, and carrot in the oil. It helps to keep the heat low and the pan covered. When the onions are soft, stir in the garlic and thyme. Be careful not to burn the garlic. Add back the rabbit, wine, tomatoes (broken up a little if whole), and potatoes. Add salt and pepper to taste. Cook covered for 45 minutes to one hour. Keep an eye on the potatoes—you want them cooked through, but not collapsing.

If you kept the heart, kidneys, and liver, fry them separately for a few minutes over medium heat with some oil or butter and a little salt and pepper. These bits of offal will be delicious, the liver particularly so, on toasted bread. Resist the temptation to add the liver to the stew, as it will give the stew a metallic taste.

36
KILL AND COOK A DEER

HOW TO HUNT A DEER

You may need a license to hunt deer depending on what country you are in. This should be considered before setting out. Also, the type of weapon you may use could be restricted; handguns are not legal for hunting in many countries. Patience will be necessary in order to hunt and kill deer successfully. They will not remain long in one place, and you will need to track them, taking care to stay downwind and to avoid making any alarming noises. It is unlikely that you will get very close to a deer. Binoculars and a rifle would be useful tools. It is preferable to shoot or kill a deer by aiming for its head and neck to avoid spoiling the meat by perforating the intestines.

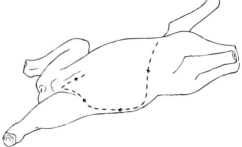

HOW TO SKIN
AND CLEAN A DEER

Start with the hind legs. Cut around the hooves and down the legs, then, using your fingers, peel back the skin. Use your hands to separate the skin from the flesh and peel the skin down the animal. Then, skin the forelegs. When you get to the neck, twist the head sharply and use your knife to cut through the remaining tissues. Remove the hide. If you want to keep the hide, clean it well of all flesh or leave it on the ground so that ants will clean it for you.

Always gut the animal as soon as possible, preferably close to the kill site, once it is safe, and far away from your chosen campsite. Lay the deer on its back, elevating the rear end up a slope or placing it on a convenient log. Then, cut carefully around the anus and tie it off so no excrement leaks out. Place the knife carefully into the hide and make a small slit to enable you to insert your fingers. Next, using your fingers to raise the skin away from the meat and as a guide, reinsert your knife and cut upward along the length of the carcass until you reach the neck. It may be easier to do this if you splay the legs outward. Roll the animal to the side. All of the intestines and internal organs should simply roll out. If you have proceeded with care, they should also be intact. If unfortunate spillage has occurred, clean the meat quickly with warm water. It is safest to cut contaminated meat away and discard it.

HOW TO MOVE A DEAD DEER

Check the carcass and discard any other organs, and then, with paper towels, pat dry the inside of the carcass. If you need to move the animal at this point and are alone, tie a rope around its head and drag it on its back to avoid collecting debris on the way. You can also carefully tie its head and legs to a pole and, with the help of a friend, carry it to your chosen destination. Hang the deer by its head when butchering, but by its feet when allowing the meat to mature. Do not leave the carcass of any animal hanging in your camp, as it will attract hungry four-legged food critics. If you wish to store the animal, tie it to a pole and suspend it between trees. This should keep it safe from most scavengers. It may be necessary to cut away the meat you will reasonably use before it goes bad and abandon the rest at the kill site.

HOW TO BUTCHER A DEER

To cut the deer into manageable pieces for transporting, storing, and cooking, do the following:

Take your hunting knife and slice the muscle connecting the front legs to the body and remove them.

To remove the back legs, cut around the large leg bone and cut the ligaments around the hip joint. Twist and bend each leg to separate and remove it.

Remove the large muscles on the spine. Break the ribs and then cut through the breaks to separate the ribs from the backbone.

Smaller pieces of meat that are still attached to the bones are suitable for soup. Larger pieces can be roasted on a spit or boiled. The tongue can be skinned and boiled. Soup can be made from the kidneys, liver, spleen, heart, and brain.

HOW TO COOK A DEER

Wild venison is not to everyone's taste, but it is safe to eat, as the bacteria on it will be killed off once it is cooked. Venison is a naturally lean meat. Remove as much fat and silverskin as possible before cooking. Too much fat on the meat will create an unpleasant taste. Removing the meat from the carcass quickly will ensure that it is tender. Soaking the meat in brine, salad dressing, or even ketchup or fruit juice will enhance the flavor. Do not add salt when cooking venison, as it prevents the meat from browning. Since you have carefully removed all the fat from the meat, you must now add another source of fat for cooking. Fat from other meat or butter can be used. If grilling or roasting venison, either wrap it in foil or baste it to avoid dryness and toughness.

RECIPE: ROAST VENISON

- Trimmed venison chuck or rump roast
- One cup (236 milliliters) water
- One cup (236 milliliters) red wine
- Cloves
- Bay leaves
- Allspice
- Onion
- Cooking oil

First, make a marinade with one cup of water, one cup of red wine, some cloves, bay leaves, allspice, and onion. If you are lacking any of these ingredients, happily substitute with fruit juice, tomatoes, and any herbs you can find, ensuring that you have about two cups of liquid.

Pour your marinade on your skinned and trimmed venison chuck or rump roast. Cover and leave in a cold place for one hour, or for two hours if possible. Remove the meat from the marinade, reserving the liquid. Brown the meat on all sides in a pot with heated oil or animal fat. Once the meat is browned, pour a half a cup of marinade over the meat and cook slowly, in a covered pot, over your fire. Check regularly and add more marinade to prevent the meat from sticking and to keep the roast moist. The liquid in the pot should be simmering. The meal should be ready to eat in about three hours.

37
KILL AND COOK A HEDGEHOG

CONSIDER HEDGEHOGS AS FOOD

Historians have uncovered recipes from as early as 6000 BC for roasted hedgehog. It should be noted that hedgehogs are protected in some countries. In the United Kingdom and in many states of the United States, it is illegal to keep them as pets or kill them because they are listed as endangered species. In other countries, it is illegal to keep them as pets or to breed them. Local laws should be referenced before you plan your menu.

WHERE HEDGEHOGS LIVE

Various species of hedgehogs live in East Africa, Europe, Asia, and in New Zealand, where they were introduced. They are not native to Australia or to the Americas. All hedgehogs like to burrow, and they eat insects, eggs, small mammals, roots, frogs, and birds. They only move around within a 120-yard (100-meter) radius of their nest, and they grow up to nine inches (23 centimeters) long and weigh two pounds (one kilogram).

HOW TO KILL A HEDGEHOG

Hedgehogs will not be found during the day and will most likely be close to a mass of broken wood or a large pile of leaves. You can trap a hedgehog easily if you leave out some tempting food, such as raw meat, insects, or worms. Throwing a box or blanket over the hedgehog will prevent it from escaping. Hedgehogs are not fast runners and have poor eyesight, but they do have a keen sense of smell, so you need to remain downwind of your trap.

HOW TO PREPARE
AND ROAST A HEDGEHOG

Once caught, the hedgehog will curl itself into a protective ball. Immersing the hedgehog in hot water will make it open up. It should then be killed by cutting its throat. Proceed to gut the animal and truss it like a chicken. That is, tie its legs together after gutting to ensure that the meat does not dry out in cooking. An alternative method is to roll the animal in clay after killing it and then bake it in the embers of the fire until the clay hardens. The spikes of the hedgehog will then remain encased in clay and you can free the soft underbelly for your meal.

ROADKILL

It is possible to use the above methods to cook a hedgehog that has already been killed by a fast-moving vehicle. In this case, it is best to ensure that the innards are not ruptured. A hedgehog's diet is such that its guts are not safe to eat. If you have witnessed the fatal car accident, you can be sure that the meat is fresh. Otherwise, it may be best to err on the side of caution and not attempt to cook the animal unless you are experienced in cooking roadkill or are very confident that the animal's blood is red, fresh, and unspoiled.

RECIPE: HEDGEHOG SPAGHETTI CARBONARA

- 18 ounces (500 grams) spaghetti
- Two tablespoons (30 milliliters) olive oil
- Nine ounces (250 grams) lean hedgehog, gutted, cleaned, and chopped into small chunks
- One medium onion, chopped
- One-half cup (125 milliliters) water
- One-quarter cup (60 milliliters) dry white wine
- Four eggs
- One-quarter cup (60 milliliters) heavy whipping cream
- Three ounces (80 grams) grated Parmesan cheese

Put eggs and cream in a bowl and beat together. Add half of the Parmesan cheese. Put onions and hedgehog chunks in a pan with olive oil on medium heat until onions are almost clear. Add wine to the pan and reduce heat to simmer gently until meat is cooked. Put pasta in boiling water with a pinch of salt. Drain the pasta when cooked. Combine it immediately with egg, cream, and cheese mix. Add hedgehog, onions, and wine (without draining the fat) and mix thoroughly. Sprinkle the remaining cheese over it and serve.

38
START AND MAINTAIN A FIRE

LIGHT YOUR FIRE

There are many methods of lighting a fire. For a more thorough discussion, look in Chapter 12, "Light a Fire," in Book One. Take out your matches from your equipment. If they are wet and unusable, then take out your flint and strike it against a saw-toothed blade to create a spark. If your flint is unavailable, hold up your magnifying glass, spectacles, camera lens, or a piece of glass to create a focused beam of sunlight on your tinder. If it is cloudy, create a hand drill or bow drill to light your tinder. If this does not work, consider opening a bullet and pouring its contents on your kindling. Bang stones together or try using your bow drill again. If fire still remains elusive, call for help or enlist the help of other members of your party. Remember with regret that this is one of those skills you should have practiced before heading out.

WHAT DOES YOUR FIRE WANT?

It is important to take a moment to consider your fire's needs. In order for your fire to perform to its fullest, it has three requirements: fuel, air, and heat. If it is deprived of any of these, it will simply go out. Keep your fire happy. Ensure that it is built in a nice, sheltered spot with plenty of fresh air and feed it well with wood.

PREPARING FOR YOUR CAMPFIRE

Lighting a fire may be a challenge in itself, but all that hard work will prove fruitless if you cannot keep your fire going. Careful site selection and some preparation before you start will reap rewards later as you sit back feeling warm and cozy next to your roaring fire.

First, find a dry, flat area away from overhanging trees, hornet's nests, and game trails that is sheltered from the wind.

Remove dry leaves from an area 12 feet (three and a half meters) in diameter and place a small circle of stones to surround your fire. These will heat and be useful for cooking later. If the ground is wet, layer it with green logs and then place stones on top of them. Choose stones that sound solid when you bang them and do not crack or they could explode when your fire heats up. Digging a small depression under your layer of stones or logs will feed your fire with more air.

Once these preparations are made, create a tepee with kindling, with your tinder in the center. Kindling can be dead wood collected from the trees nearby, cardboard, or wood that you have doused with oil, wax, or gasoline. Tinder may be absorbent cotton (cotton wool), bird down, dry grass, resin from trees, dry pine needles, or evergreen cones. It must be completely dry. Once the kindling is lit, add dry wood to the tepee. The logs will fall inward as they burn. This fire will work even if some of the wood is green.

KEEPING YOUR FIRE GOING AGAINST THE ODDS

You may find yourself battling with the elements to try to keep your fire lit, or to make it at all. If it is very windy, consider constructing your fire next to a large boulder or against a felled wet log to protect it. Simply lay your kindling up against the log with the tinder behind and build it up gradually with dry wood once it is lit. In wet weather, find the most sheltered spot you can find. All members of the group should be employed to gather firewood, which should be stored close to the fire and kept covered to keep it as dry as possible. Very green wood may need to be dried

near the fire before use to prevent the fire from extinguishing.

In stormy weather or near the sea, consider digging a trench about one foot (30 centimeters) deep, two feet (60 centimeters) wide, and three feet (one meter) long. Layer the trench with stones and light your fire on top. This type of fire is very convenient when cooking, as meat can be skewered and laid over the pit.

FIRE FOR WARMTH

If keeping warm is your primary concern, try to locate your fire so that rocks, logs, or sand dunes are near enough to reflect the heat back to you. If this is not possible, you can quickly create such a reflector with whatever materials are at hand. They may also be used as a windbreak. Do not use overly flammable materials or build the reflector too close to the fire. If you only have time and resources for one such structure, sit opposite it. If you have more time, you may wish to build a second one behind you as well.

FUEL FOR YOUR FIRE

Once your fire is lit, you must keep it well fed. While tinder and kindling must be dry and easily combustible, the main fuel for your fire can burn more slowly. Any dry wood or dead wood, animal fats, coal, pinecones, dry clothing, or leaves will suffice. It is a good idea to poke the fire at regular intervals to keep the fuel burning evenly and to add fuel.

39
MAKE A TORCH

Making a torch in the wild is not hard, but it is likely to be trickier than most movies suggest. How effective your torch is will depend on the materials you use and whether or not you have fuel. A well-made torch will last more than 20 minutes and will not spray you with sparks and burning material as you walk.

START WITH A STICK

Your first step to torch making is to select a stick thick enough to be easy to grip and long enough so that the lit end can be held away from your clothes and face; at least two feet (60 centimeters) long is best. Using hard, green wood for the stick will prevent it from catching fire accidentally, which is preferable.

TYPES OF TORCHES

You will need to wrap the top of your torch with something flammable. You can take some unwanted clothing, rip it into strips, and wrap it around the stick. If you find yourself equipped with an overabundance of toilet paper in camp, you can wrap the top with this. You will need a couple of rolls at least.

Another method is to strip bark from a tree, wrap it in a cone shape, and tie it to the top of your stick. Alternating green and dry bark will prevent excessive sparks. Most bark will then need to be filled with dry grass, leaves, or dry pieces of bark. If you find birch bark, you will not need to pad it out. Simply wrap the bark quite tightly around the stick and tie it on with vine, string, or wire.

Leaving some space for air to circulate is beneficial for all types of bark torch.

SOAKING YOUR TORCH

You then need to soak the top of the torch in a fuel that will slow down the burning. Any type of fat, either vegetable or boiled-down animal fat, will work well. Fuel from your vehicle, tree sap, or even lip balm will also make effective fuel. It will be necessary to soak the torch tip for up to 20 minutes, depending on its type. It may then take a couple of minutes to light your torch. It is a good idea to prepare your torches in daylight and have them soaking and ready to light from your campfire should the need arise.

MORE PERMANENT SOLUTIONS

You may feel the need to make a more permanent torch for your campsite. If this is the case, a metal pole that can be driven into the ground or carried is a good idea. A thick, green piece of wood may also be used, but may need to be occasionally replaced when it dries out and becomes a fire hazard.

Take two used tin cans, one slightly wider than the other. Pour fuel or oil into the larger can. Bore a good hole into the bottom of the smaller can and feed through a cloth to act as a wick. Place the small can on top of the larger can so that the fuel is trapped inside and the wick is pointing up. Use whatever is available to tie the cans together. Then, tie the cans to the top of the pole and light the wick. You can also make this type of torch with only one can, but there is a danger of spilling burning oil on yourself, your campsite, or others, so use caution.

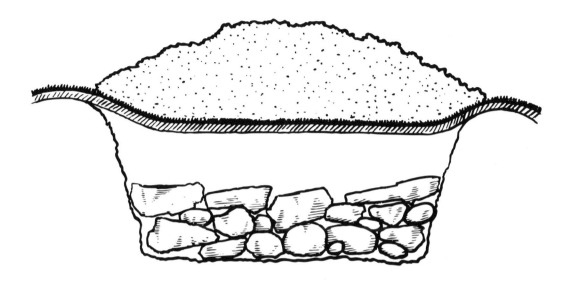

40
BUILD A PIT OVEN

HOW TO BUILD A PIT OVEN

The basic idea of a pit oven is based on the fact that stone retains heat, so when you bury extremely hot stones next to some very well-wrapped food, the heat from the stones cooks the food. Pit ovens have an edge over open fires because they require no supervision once you have constructed them and allow you to cook a large amount of food together. Pit cooking traps heat and moisture inside, producing food that is exceptionally moist and extremely delicious. A final advantage of pit ovens is their remarkable fuel efficiency; they use much less wood than an open fire to cook the same amount of food. Follow the simple steps in this section and you'll be burying your dinner in no time.

GET DIGGING

Your first step is to dig your pit—no surprises there. Overall, it needs to be about two to three times wider than the food you're going to cook, and about a foot (30 centimeters) deep. Making it any bigger just gives you more work than you need. Keep the excavated earth in a pile nearby.

Next, line the inside of the pit with stones. Flat ones are better than round ones for the base of the oven because they create a more even cooking surface, but the most important thing is to avoid wet stones taken from a river or another water source, as the absorbed moisture can cause them to explode during cooking.

Build and light a small fire on top of your stones. Add twigs and branches as necessary, and spread the fire along the length of the pit to ensure that all the stones are being heated thoroughly. The hot stones, rather than the fire itself, will do the cooking. Leave the fire for about an hour to allow the stones to get really, really hot.

PREPARE YOUR MEAL

While your stones are heating up, prepare your food for cooking. Pit ovens can be used to cook anything that you can cook in a normal oven, including fish, meat, potatoes, and even bread or biscuits. If you're cooking a large piece of meat, or even a whole animal you've hunted, like a deer, wild boar, or rabbit, you may want to joint it first to ensure it is cooked thoroughly and evenly. Potatoes can simply be buried whole with their skins on. Traditionally, food would be wrapped in large leaves or sandwiched between two beds of edible greens—such as watercress, mint, or dandelion—before cooking as protection from the dirt and embers. Of course, these days you can use aluminum foil if you prefer.

Once the stones are hot, sweep the embers to one side and lower your dinner into the oven. Cover it with a thin layer of leaves and sprinkle the whole thing with water. This water will produce steam during the cooking process.

BURY AND WAIT

Now all that remains to do is to return the earth you dug out earlier to seal the oven. Before you do this, laying something reasonably large and flat over the leaves will form another barrier between the dirt and your dinner and simplify the removal process. An old piece of wet fabric is ideal, because you can leave the edges at ground level as you replace the soil, but other options include some planks of wood, some old carpet, or slabs of bark. Don't use a plastic bag—it will melt. Once you've laid down your final barrier and replaced the soil, then go and do something else for a couple of hours until your food is ready.

When you think the time has come, carefully dig up the oven, take out your cooked treasure, unwrap, and enjoy.

41
WASH AND CLEAN

DIRT IS GOOD

Regardless of what your mother once told you, dirt can be good for you when you are enjoying the outdoor life. A nice layer of dirt on your skin may protect you from insect bites, sunburn, and even germs. Overwashing may leave your skin soft and more exposed to the elements. It is always a good idea to use soap and warm water to clean your hands before administering first aid. Otherwise, wash sparingly.

SOAP

If you are running out of soap, keep whatever supply you have in case it is needed to clean wounds. If you are determined to wash with soap, you can always produce more using what you find in the wild, a fire, a couple of containers, and some cloth for straining.

The main ingredients for soap are lye and fat. Animal fat can be used and wood ash is a good source for making lye. Dried palm branches, oak, apple tree wood, or even dried banana peels, cocoa pods, and dry seaweed can be used to make lye water.

METHOD

First, chop up your animal fat and cook slowly, adding water to prevent it from sticking to the pot. Once it has liquefied, pour it out to harden in a waiting container. Next, take the wood ash you have already collected (from the remains of last night's fire), place in a container with water, and then strain it.

To strain the wood ash, take a waterproof container and make holes in the bottom. Cover the holes with a layer of pebbles or gravel and top this with a layer of straw. Fill the container with the ashes, leaving space at the top to add the water. Then, fill with rainwater or water from a nearby stream. Place a bowl under the container to catch the lye water, being careful not to drip any outside.

Add this water to the grease, remembering that one part lye water should be used for every two parts fat. Using too much lye will make soap that dries out and irritates the skin.

Boil this mixture well. Be careful not to inhale the fumes or let the hot liquid touch your skin. Once the mixture has thickened, add pine needles or eucalyptus leaves, as this will make the soap antiseptic. Then, pour it out into containers to harden and cut into bars.

SAFETY WHEN WORKING WITH LYE

Lye is corrosive; it is also used as a drain unblocker, so it is best not to allow it on your bare skin. It may be fatal if swallowed or cause blindness if splashed in the eyes. Use gloves and glasses if possible. The soaked ash may be buried. Any unused lye water should be disposed of very carefully.

GOOD CAMP HYGIENE

All of your equipment should be kept clean and dry at all times. Your eating and cooking utensils should be washed immediately after use. Uneaten food should be placed in sealed containers or disposed of away from your camp. Any fish or animals trapped or killed should be cleaned and cut next to traps and not in camp. Leave meat at a kill site if you will not be able to eat it before it spoils. You do not wish to attract insects or predators to your campsite. All members of your party, regardless of their age or infirmity, should be given tasks to ensure that your campsite is kept clean. Should you be in a humid or tropical climate, do not attempt to store any meat or uneaten food, as it could result in food poisoning.

DOWNSTREAM

When planning your camp, ensure that you have a water collection place nearby. Wash your food and kitchen utensils farther away from camp. Your own washing area should be even farther downstream, while the toilet area must be farthest downstream or downhill from camp. This should prevent you from fouling your own water supply and help keep you healthy and clean.

42
DIG A TOILET

Depending on the length of your excursion, you may quite possibly need to answer the call of nature. Indeed, even if you are only planning to spend a single night in your camp, some form of toilet should be considered, if only for hygienic reasons.

SELECTING A SPOT

When selecting a site for your toilet, make sure that it is approximately 200 feet (60 meters) downwind from your camp. This will prevent any lingering scents from infiltrating your base. Make sure that it is also approximately the same distance from any water source.

Try to select a site that receives plenty of sunlight and consists of organic soil. These factors will assist in decomposition. You may also prefer the privacy afforded at the foot of a hill or behind a bountiful bush.

PLAN OF ACTION

If the toilet is for single use, dig a hole about six to eight inches (15 to 20 centimeters) deep using a small garden trowel. Return the freshly dug soil to the hole after use.

If the toilet is for repeated use, dig a hole about two to three feet (60 to 90 centimeters) deep using a shovel. Use logs to build a wall around the entrance to the hole to a comfortable sitting height. This will provide you with a seat. Throw a handful of soil over any waste added to your toilet. Should it start to smell badly or become quite full, simply cover it up with soil and dig a new toilet.

COVERING YOUR TOILET

It is best to create a lid for your toilet, as this will limit flies and unpleasant smells in the area. The lid can be made of wood or any material readily available.

PRIVACY

You may wish to carefully select an area with some natural screens in the form of trees and bushes. You can also erect a makeshift tent over your toilet or hang some material from a nearby tree to make a privacy screen. This privacy screen should not be used in place of a cover, as it will not deter flies. You will simply find yourself sitting inside a fly-infested tent on your camp toilet.

LEAVING YOUR TOILET

Remember to fill your toilet with soil when you are moving camp. If it is deep enough, you may bury unwanted organic rubbish here, too.

URINAL

If you desire a separate urinal, then dig a small hole, about two feet (60 centimeters) deep, and layer the bottom with small stones. Tear a piece of bark from a nearby tree and curl and tie the bark into a cone shape with an opening at the narrow end. Place the cone onto the stones and refill the hole loosely with more stones and top with soil. Ensure that the cone is securely upright and take aim.

When leaving the area, simply remove the cone, bury it, and fill the hole with more soil. Make sure you choose a site that is away from your water supply and is not in a deep depression or close to camp. If the cone no longer drains, dig a new urinal, as you have limited the soaking capacity of the nearby soil.

BOOK FOUR

SURVIVING ADVERSITY

43
PREPARE FOR AN EMERGENCY: SURVIVAL PACK

You have packed up your backpack or car with all the essentials to make your trip comfortable and fun. An emergency survival pack is necessary in case it turns out to be a more harrowing experience.

Within your emergency pack, you should bring materials for the following:

• First aid
• Fire lighting
• Food procurement
• Emergency rations
• Signaling help
• Shelter
• Finding your way

Ideally, these items should be stored, not in your bag or vehicle, but on your person. If a sudden flood, accident, or animal attack causes you to be separated from your camp and supplies, you will still have your emergency pack at the ready.

STORAGE

These items should be dry and sealed in a handy tin or pouch tied to your belt or slung over your shoulder. The tin or pouch should not be big, bulky, or heavy. Do not duplicate items. For example, you can buy a small compass for your wrist that is self-illuminating. Consider breaking matches in half to save space. Put bulky first aid items elsewhere, simply carrying enough in your emergency pack for immediate use. A mirror is a handy item for signaling for help, but the lid of your tin can be polished and used for this, too.

FIRST AID

For example, a bear has chased you from your camp. You are lost and have scratched your hands and face in the scramble to escape unmauled. Your first aid kit should have some painkillers, water sterilization tablets, soap, Band-Aids, and butterfly sutures to deal with your injuries. The condom in your kit will serve as water storage.

FINDING YOUR WAY

In your sprint away from the bear, you have lost your bearings. Take note of your surroundings and check your compass, which is either tucked into your survival pouch or on your wrist.

SHELTER

You have given up hope of a return to camp until morning. You have packed a knife, a flexible saw, and a survival bag to keep you insulated. Survival bags when new will take up no more room than a large, well-folded plastic bag, so do not be tempted to travel without one. You proceed to make a shelter using materials nearby.

FIRE

You have found dry matches and cotton in your pack. The lip balm in your pack can be used as fuel for a torch. You use your torch to find firewood and build a bright, smoky fire.

RATIONS

You open your emergency rations, which include dried meat, fruit, nuts, and chocolate, and enjoy a supper for one.

MORE FOOD

It is morning. You are still unsure of which direction to travel and are safe where you are. You use the trap wire and set a trapline. You go to a nearby river with the hooks and line from your pack and catch a fish for breakfast. Then, you sit back and sew your clothes, which were ripped in your flight, using the needles and thread you packed.

STILL WAITING TO BE RESCUED

You walk to higher ground, staying close to your makeshift camp, and fire the flare from your emergency pack. Then, you go back to enjoy your cozy fire and await rescue.

44
PRIORITIES IN AN EMERGENCY SITUATION

TRY TO AVOID EMERGENCY SITUATIONS

Good planning and packing are essential in any expedition and should eliminate the possibility of many mishaps, such as getting lost or running out of food. In addition, monitoring weather reports and keeping abreast of meteorological warnings may help you avoid earthquakes, volcanoes, floods, hurricanes, or the like, which may hamper the enjoyment of your trip.

DO NOT PANIC

Should you encounter an emergency, do not panic. Prioritizing is very important so that you and your party can come away unscathed. Air, water, food, and shelter are the four necessities of survival that you should keep in mind if you become isolated or separated from your supplies. A person can go only a few minutes without air, and a few days without water. Finding water should therefore be your first priority, assuming a lack of air is not a problem.

RATION WATER

If you are stranded and awaiting rescue and are unable to move or find water, it is essential that you take steps to ration the water you have and prevent dehydration. The human body loses between three and a half and five and a half pints (two to three liters) of water each day. If you have a supply of two pints (one liter) of water, ration it by taking small sips and drinking one-third of it a day. If on the final day you still haven't been rescued, ration the water further into thirds, taking half of this daily ration at midday and the rest at night.

In order to make this rationing of water more effective, you should do your best to help your body retain the fluids you have. Do not move around and try to stay cool. Eat as little as possible, as eating increases the rate of dehydration. Avoid alcohol. Do not talk unnecessarily and breathe through your nose, as this will help avoid unpleasant mouth dryness.

LISTEN TO THE RADIO

Should extreme weather or any natural disaster be a possibility, keep in tune with local news reports. This could give you some much-needed information about when and in what direction to evacuate. All of your group members should stay together and have an agreed-upon place to regroup if separated.

MEDICAL EMERGENCY

It is always advisable to get expert medical assistance. When enjoying the great outdoors, though, this is not always possible. There are also instances when quick action is necessary. The ABCs of first aid are airway, breathing, and circulation. First, check that the airway is not blocked, that the person is breathing, and that they have a pulse. It is important in the case of multiple injured parties to assess who needs attention first. The person who is screaming the loudest and bleeding may not be as injured as the person lying quietly unconscious. Take no longer than one minute to assess who should be treated first, using the basis of whether the situation is life-threatening, urgent but not life-threatening, or not urgent. Having a properly equipped medical kit packed and having all of your party trained in first aid will be very beneficial in this situation.

GET SAFE, GET HELP, GET FOOD, AND STAY SAFE

Should you find yourself in a natural disaster or an extreme weather event, it is important to stick to a plan, stick together, and remember your survival priorities. First, you must ensure that you and your group are safe from harm. This may mean fleeing to water or to a clearing in the trees to escape a fire. It may mean moving to high ground, abandoning your stalled car, or tying yourself and your supplies to the chimney of a roof to avoid a flood. Should an official evacuation take place due to a hurricane, volcano, or impending earthquake, do not hesitate to cooperate. Once you are safe from harm, you must do everything possible to draw attention to your location so you can be rescued. This may mean lighting a fire, hanging out bright blankets, or using flares, whistles, or torches. If you are in a group, take turns to remain alert and call for help if necessary. Once these first two conditions are met, you should look for food and supplies, or make careful note of what you have and then ration accordingly. If satisfying the first condition of a safe location necessitates that you move rather than remain in one place, it is essential that you are sure of the direction you are moving in and your destination. It is usually a better option to remain in one place and wait for help to come to you. Do not risk moving yourself and your party unnecessarily. Once you have found a safe place, stay there.

CONTINGENCY PLAN

In order to deal with any emergencies you may encounter—either due to accident, illness, or natural disasters—a contingency plan is necessary. Everyone in the group should have their own small survival pack that they carry with them. A discussion of what action to take in the case of extreme weather or other mishap should take place before you set out. This will eliminate the need for discussion and democratic voting when quick action is needed.

Forest fire danger sign

45
SOME OF THE SURVIVAL SKILLS

There are many survival skills, in some of which you may already be well versed, and others you may never have had occasion to use. Some may be practiced and mastered, such as fire making and foraging. Others, such as first aid or defending against predators, you may learn only in theory and be happy never to have occasion to test your knowledge.

Basic survival skills include emergency first aid, making a shelter, making a fire without matches, procuring safe water in the wild, foraging for food, hunting for food, surviving in varying terrains and climates, avoiding and defending against predators, identifying and treating animal, reptile, and insect bites, and living in the wild. Other chapters of this book discuss these survival skills in detail.

Some more specific survival skills that you may need include how to escape from a raging forest fire, how to survive a flood, how to cope in a hurricane or tornado, and how to react if there is an earthquake.

FOREST FIRE
Should you find yourself in a forest when a fire starts, try to assess the situation calmly. If your campfire has spread to surrounding woodland, it is best to attempt to smother it using whatever blankets or coverings you have. If this is unsuccessful, or if the fire is not of your making and of a larger magnitude, you will need to take more extreme action.

Before you run away, assess if the fire is spreading in your direction. Do not remove your clothing, as it will protect you from the heat. Move in the opposite direction of the wind and smoke if possible. If the fire is spreading in a wide front toward you, then head for the nearest firebreak or large clearing in the trees, or for a river if there is one nearby. Do not make for high ground, as fire spreads faster uphill. If you are able to get to the already burnt and cleared area with relative ease and only some singeing, you can consider it as a last resort. It will require you to run toward the fire.

Once you have effectively escaped from the fire, seek medical help immediately to treat any minor burns and any injuries sustained due to smoke inhalation.

FLOOD
Because floods have many causes, it is best to keep up-to-date with weather reports and avoid flood plains during torrential downpours. If preventive techniques prove ineffective and

you are indeed caught in a flood, you will need to make for higher ground.

If you are camping in the wild and are making for higher ground as floodwaters rise, you should be aware that all of the animals will be joining you. Try to keep out of their way, as they may not be proceeding in a calm, orderly fashion.

If you are driving, do not attempt to go through water that is higher than your tires. If your car stalls in floodwater, get out and leave it. If the flood worsens, your car may be swept away with you in it. It is unlikely to remain upright if this happens.

If you are inside a building when flooding occurs, do not go outside. Gather all water, food, warm clothes, and emergency first aid and signaling supplies and head upstairs or out on the roof. How high you need to go will depend on the level of flooding. It is safer to turn off electricity and gas in the building. Remember that floodwater carries debris and hides obstacles and can travel at high speeds. Do not attempt to wade or swim in floodwater. You should sit tight, blow on your whistle, and await rescue.

HURRICANE OR TORNADO

A hurricane, also known as a typhoon, is simply a wind of very high speed. It can cause extensive property damage and flooding and, if you are unprepared, present a threat to your life.

A tornado occurs when wind turns in a spiral, gaining speeds of more than 300 mph (480 kph). Once a tornado touches ground, it destroys almost everything in its path. Tornados usually happen at certain times of the year and are usually forecast. However, it is not possible to predict the exact timing or path of a tornado.

If you are inside a solid building with a cellar or basement, go there immediately. It is unsafe either to drive or walk around in a hurricane or tornado. If there is no cellar, then stand underneath the stairs. Do not stand near the chimney breast or anywhere near windows.

In a hurricane, you should close all the windows. It was once thought that leaving windows slightly open during a hurricane could prevent your house from imploding from the lower air pressure of the storm. This would only occur if your house were airtight, which is not likely even with all the doors and windows closed. Flying debris in the storm, or high wind velocity hitting your house, will create cracks in windows and walls and may even remove your roof, creating a great deal of ventilation. Do not waste time opening windows. Should the storm include lightning, make sure you are not standing next to any windows or tall trees and, if you are still outside, do not hold metal. It is better to stay low to the ground to avoid being hit. If you have time, try to find a nice, dry insulating material to sit on and make sure that no part of your body is touching the ground. A direct hit with lightning can result in heart failure.

The best survival technique in the case of hurricanes and tornados is to move out of their path or, even better, out of the area altogether.

EARTHQUAKE

Minor earthquakes occur all over the world and are usually not life-threatening. If you are traveling in parts of the world where earthquakes are frequent, such as Japan, Indonesia, New Zealand, or the Pacific Coast of the Americas, you should listen to local broadcasts. It is possible that you will receive a warning about a large quake that will allow you to evacuate safely.

If you receive an earthquake warning but are unable to leave the area in time, take some precautions. If you are in a strong, well-built structure, turn off the gas and electricity and secure stores of water and food. Go to the cellar, if there is one. A doorframe is another option. Do not stand next to any glass mirrors, windows, glass-fronted cabinets, or cabinets full of glasses. If you are in a large building with an elevator, do not use the elevator.

If you are driving when an earthquake happens, try to bring your car to a safe stop, curl up into a ball, and wait inside until it is all over.

If you happen to be walking around, calmly fling yourself on the ground. It is better if you land away from tall trees or unstable-looking buildings. Running around is not advisable, however tempting it may be.

Earthquakes can trigger tsunamis, floods, and mudslides, and usually cause disruption in the local water, food, and electricity supplies. Due to the risk of a tsunami, it is best to leave the beach promptly after an earthquake. Standing at the base of a hill is also not a good idea, in case of a mudslide. Rivers and riverbeds should also be avoided in case landslides upstream cause flooding.

46
FIRE A FLARE

If you find yourself in need of rescue, you may need to use a flare. Red flares signal an emergency. There are many types of flares, including those that you hold in your hand and aerial flares shot from guns. Parachute flares will hang in the air for up to 30 seconds. Flares are more visible when it is dark. All flares will indicate your position and can be seen from the air or by other vessels at sea. Handheld types will pinpoint your position most precisely. All flares should be used with caution.

FLARE GUN

You will find firing a flare gun easier if you have fired a traditional firearm, as the principle is the same—you simply pull the trigger. The main difference is that you point the flare gun vertically in the air. As in a regular firearm, the hammer will hit a detonating cap that fires and ignites the flare.

HANDHELD FLARE

These should be used with caution, and preferably while wearing gloves. Stand in a clear, elevated position away from dry, flammable materials. If using a flare on a boat, stand with your arm over the side. Follow the instructions and activate the firing mechanism. Move your hand away from the top of the flare, as it will light in one or two seconds and will become extremely hot. Stay very still and keep your body as far away from the flare as possible. It should burn for about a minute. Try to avoid looking directly at the flare, as you could find yourself temporarily blinded. When the flare stops, it will still be very hot. Do not discard it by dropping it to the bottom of your dinghy or in a bed of dry twigs in the forest.

HOW TO USE A FLARE

If you are at sea, try to wait until another vessel or a plane is in sight. Then fire two flares, allowing about one minute between shots. The first flare will attract your rescuers' attention and the second will help them pinpoint your position. If you see a commercial plane, or if the other vessel is too far away and it is during the day, resist wasting your flares. Flares can be seen up to five miles away at night by surface vessels at sea.

OTHER USES

Flares are not fireworks. They should not be used in a desperate attempt to light a fire or as a makeshift torch.

Flares have been used in self-defense by hikers who were attacked by a dangerous animal, although this is not their intended purpose. A flare may cause injury to a charging animal, or, if you miss, may simply anger it. Flares have been known to scare away charging bears, although bear pepper spray is more suitable for this purpose. Firing a flare horizontally is not recommended. It will be hot and could very easily set fire to the surrounding area when it lands. Never point a flare at another person or use a flare in or near your tent.

OTHER TYPES OF FLARES

If you are traveling at sea, you are required to always carry flares of varying types. Smoke flares are much more visible during the day. You can buy smoke flares in orange, which clearly distinguishes them from campfire smoke. They light for less than one minute and are visible for five miles during the day. They are a better option than colored flares during the day.

A mixture of aerial, parachute, and handheld flares, smoke flares, and different colored flares can be used to attract maximum attention.

47
RESCUE STRATEGIES

It is important to be well versed in various rescue strategies for your expedition. If traveling by sea, know how to signal for help. If hiking on a mountain, understand mountain rescue procedures. If entering jungle terrain or isolated areas, know how to signal to an aircraft for rescue. Know how to use flares and radios, and how to draw attention to yourself in order to get rescued.

AT SEA

Depending on where you are sailing, you will need to comply with local coast guard regulations regarding carrying flares and other equipment for safety and to enable rescue. Should your boat be disabled but still floating, you will be able to stay safe while signaling for rescue. If you are forced to abandon your vessel in a raft, try to make for shore. It is easier to survive and easier to signal for rescue on land than it is on the open sea. Do not waste your flares. Fire two in succession only when you see a vessel on the horizon. Use smoke flares in daylight. If a helicopter drops a winch to rescue you, always allow it to hit the water or boat before touching it or you will get an electric shock.

IN THE WILDERNESS

Regardless of whether you are in a forest, jungle, or desert, you need to be visible in order to get rescued. Do not make a camp under tree cover. Use flares if you have them, but keep them for when you see an aircraft or people on the horizon.

Use whatever materials you have to make your position clear by air and land. Use rocks or available material to mark out the letters SOS on the ground, making each letter about 30 feet (10 meters) long and nine feet (three meters) wide.

Light a fire and collect smoke-creating materials that you can place on your fire to attract attention. In a forest, damp leaves or moss will create white smoke, which will stand out against vegetation and attract the attention of other hikers or aircraft. In the desert, pour oil or place tires on the fire to create black smoke.

If your vehicle has broken down or crashed, see if you can move pieces of it to visible areas. Mount mirrors or any reflective materials around your camp to attract attention. You may even wish to set fire to your vehicle to attract attention.

RESCUE FROM FLOOD

If you are stranded on a roof following a tsunami or flash flood, use bright-colored blankets or sheets to attract the attention of rescuers. At night, consider banging, shouting, or using whistles to attract attention if rescuers are nearby and you have no torch.

TRAVELING

If you are not safe remaining where you are, you should not travel blindly. Use a compass, the sun, or stars to determine your direction of travel. Leave markers behind showing your direction of travel and written details of your emergency and who is in your party. Try to remain on a path or near a road or follow a river or stream, as this way you are more likely to be rescued.

SIGNALS

It is helpful to know some internationally recognized signals to aid your rescue. If you know Morse code, use a rag tied to a stick. Dots and dashes can be shown by swinging the rag to the right or left respectively with exaggerated figure-of-eight movements. For clarity, do not do this too fast. If a small aircraft is nearby or a helicopter is over your position, body signals may be effective. Stand with both arms outstretched to ask for mechanical help if your car has broken down, for example. Two arms raised in the air indicate that you wish to be rescued. Avoid waving with one arm, as this means all is well.

The SOS signal is three short, three long, and then three short signals.

48
TREAT ILLNESSES AND INJURIES

You are enjoying your excursion into the wild when you are beset by a minor tragedy in the guise of illness or injury to a member of your party, or worse, yourself. A well-prepared adventurer need not give in to hopeless despair and may simply use this opportunity to try out some survival skills and practice first aid.

ASSESS THE SITUATION

The first thing to do is take a calm look at the victim or victims. If there is more than one injured person, you will need to decide whom to treat first. Personal preference is not the best guide here. Anyone who is choking, not breathing, lacking a pulse, or suffering arterial bleeding should be treated first. Try not to panic, as this will only cause your patients distress. First, treat those not breathing or without a pulse, then those who are bleeding, then those with fractures, and finally those suffering from shock. It may happen that one unfortunate victim has more than one ailment. Use your best judgment and enlist helpers if possible.

ILLNESS

It will probably not be possible to diagnose the illness with any degree of certainty.

Your priority will be to keep the patient's temperature at an optimum level. Have the patient lie comfortably in a dry shelter or tent and ensure that they are kept cool if they have a fever. If you are in a cold climate, remember that illness will make the patient more susceptible to hypothermia, so guard against this. Regardless of the symptoms, make sure that dehydration does not occur. If the patient is not vomiting or suffering from diarrhea and you have a course of antibiotics in your first aid kit, administer them. Administer analgesics to help relieve any pain or fever. Read all medicine labels carefully. Have someone keep track of all measures and medicines taken so that you can pass this information on to medical professionals.

INJURY

As with illness, the patient should be placed in a tent or shelter and kept warm. Fluids should be administered regularly. In many cases, such as a spinal injury, moving the patient will cause more harm. Therefore, do not move an injured person unless you are sure that moving them is safe. In the case of a fracture, do your best to immobilize the injury before moving. In the case of wounds, bandage them and stop the bleeding before moving the patient. If an injury has occurred in a limb, try to elevate it. Do not allow the injured person to move around. Shock, pain, or blood loss may result in dizziness or make them faint, which in turn may lead to further injury from a fall.

Should an injury to the head occur, proceed with caution. If the injury is severe, you should assume a spinal injury has also occurred. Do not wash or remove debris from a deep head wound; simply cover with a sterile dressing and call for help. If a person is unconscious but is breathing and has a pulse, a brain or spinal injury is possible and they should not be moved.

If anyone in your party has received even a light bang on the head, watch out for the following symptoms, which could indicate a brain injury: sudden drowsiness, abnormal behavior or speech, a severe headache, a stiff neck, loss of consciousness, or vomiting more than once. Even if these symptoms occur hours or days later, you should be concerned.

SHOCK

You should be aware that many people suffer from shock as a result of injury. It is also possible for onlookers to suffer from shock. Signs of shock include dizziness, rapid pulse, clammy skin, vomiting, gray-looking skin, and pale lips. The patient may also lose consciousness. To treat shock, get the sufferer to lie down and elevate their legs by about 12 inches (30 centimeters). Try to remain calm so that they will be calm. Cover them with a blanket and do not feed them.

49
TREAT DEHYDRATION AND SUNBURN

First, you must recognize the symptoms. Early signs of dehydration are thirst, a decrease in the frequency of urination, and a dry mouth. These symptoms will be followed by an inability to sweat or cry, as the body will try to retain fluid. As symptoms persist, they will become more severe. Muscle cramps, nausea, and even vomiting may occur. As your blood volume decreases, the body increases blood pressure to ensure that vital organs get blood. This may result in heart palpitations. All of the above are likely to make the patient feel light-headed and weak. If they still fail to take in any fluid, coma and eventual death will result. These symptoms will progress over three days, depending on temperature and humidity.

Sunburn is usually first noticed due to glowing pink or redness of the skin and a feeling of localized heat. There may also be irritation or a desire to scratch the area. If the patient scratches the area, it will cause discomfort or pain, depending on the severity of the sunburn and the sensitivity of the skin.

TREAT DEHYDRATION

As prevention is better than a cure, you and your group members should endeavor to take in about eight glasses of water or other fluids per day. This should be increased when taking exercise or if you are in a hot, humid environment. Supplement fluid intake with fresh fruit and vegetables and limit your intake of salty food.

At the first signs of dehydration, move the sufferer to a cool area to reduce the risk of heat stroke and have them remain still, preferably lying down in case they feel faint. Apply cool cloths to the unfortunate person's neck, wrists, upper arms, and inner thighs. Then, get them to drink water or juice in small sips. Watermelon may also be given if you happen to have some handy. If they vomit, wait a few minutes and try more fluid. If you yourself are thirsty, remember to drink. If dehydration has reached a point where the victim feels faint or is vomiting, seek expert medical attention so that a coma or death can be prevented.

TREAT SUNBURN

If you are the victim, the first step is to get out of the sun to prevent further sunburn. Then, take some pain-relieving medication; one that is anti-inflammatory will be most effective. Your next aim is to cool your skin down. Try as many of the following as possible:

- Take a cool shower and allow yourself to air dry. Use no soap.
- Take a cool bath. This is gentler if you have developing blisters.
- Dampen material and apply to your skin for 30 minutes.
- If you can find an aloe vera plant nearby, cut a leaf, scoop out the gel-like substance, and gently apply it to your skin. Do not rub it in. Reapply as needed.
- Apply a cream suitable for sunburn.
- If you have no cream, make strong tea, allow it to cool, and then dab it on your sore skin.
- If you have no painkillers, beat egg whites until stiff and apply them to your skin. Cover yourself with clothes immediately to keep the remedy in place.
- Leave blisters alone and unpopped to avoid pain and infection.
- If you do pop a blister, apply antibacterial cream and do not touch it with unwashed hands.
- If broken blisters start to smell or ooze yellow pus, they are infected and need to be cleaned thoroughly. You may need antibiotic cream to treat this effectively.

Aloe vera plant

- Do not peel off shedding skin or unsightly skin flaps left over from blisters.
- Wear loose clothes over the affected area.
- Wear a sunscreen with a high SPF on the affected area.
- Once the initial irritation has passed, help heal the skin by drinking a lot of water and applying a lot of moisturizer.

Remember that sunburn occurs due to overexposure of your skin to the sun and is very avoidable with a cunning use of clothing, hats, and sunscreen.

50
TREAT DIARRHEA, VOMITING, AND FEVER

Diarrhea, vomiting, and fever are unpleasant and debilitating to the sufferer, especially if they all occur at the same time.

DIARRHEA

You have diarrhea if you pass more than 10 ounces (300 grams) of loose stools in 24 hours. If it lasts more than one or two weeks, it is considered chronic and is probably due to improper diet, food intolerance, or a serious illness. Most diarrhea lasts only a few days and is due to infection or bacteria in water and food. It can be passed to others as a result of poor hygiene. Avoid this unpleasant illness by taking care to wash your hands regularly around food and after visiting the toilet and always drink safe water. Contaminated food will often have a regular appearance and taste, so take care to cook and store food hygienically.

Symptoms include frequent watery bowel movements, stomach pains, vomiting, fever, and dehydration.

How to Treat Diarrhea

There are many remedies available for diarrhea; most will simply replace needed salts and sugars to the body to avoid an electrolyte imbalance. If you have no remedy, then drink plenty of fluids, as you will be at risk of dehydration. Ensure that your urine is a light yellow color. Eat something salty, assuming you are not vomiting. Add sugar and salt to your drinking water.

You may be in serious trouble if you notice any blood or mucus in your bowel movements. If you are unable to drink fluids due to vomiting, you will get dehydrated quickly, and you will need medical help if this persists for 12 hours. If you are drowsy or showing any signs of dehydration, or if you are quite old or very young, you should also be more concerned.

Once symptoms stop, eat normally and avoid dairy products for two days.

VOMITING

This often accompanies diarrhea, but may also occur on its own. Vomiting is the forceful expulsion of the contents of your stomach through the mouth or nose. It may be caused by a viral or bacterial infection or by food poisoning. Chronic ongoing vomiting may indicate a more serious illness or stomach irritation due to food intolerance or an allergy.

How to Treat Vomiting

Stop eating, but keep taking in small amounts of fluids to prevent dehydration. Try to stay cool and lie down. Vomiting can be accompanied by a feeling of weakness or fainting. Apply cool, wet cloths to your neck, face, chest, and upper arms. This will help with nausea and slow down dehydration.

Antiemetic drugs will stop nausea and vomiting. If you are far away from medical help and suffering from chronic nausea, try taking antihistamines, as these may also work as antiemetics.

Once vomiting has stopped, gradually increase your fluid intake until your urine is a pale yellow color. Once you have achieved this, you can start to eat. Include something salty and add some sugar to your water.

Vomiting causes the sufferer to sweat and increases the heart rate, and may result in palpitations if symptoms are severe and persistent. If the patient is intoxicated or unconscious, vomit may be aspirated or enter the respiratory tract. This may lead to asphyxiation and death or cause pneumonia. Seek expert medical help if you suspect this has occurred, or if dehydration occurs or blood appears in the vomit.

FEVER

Fever is said to occur when normal body temperature, usually around 98.6 degrees Fahrenheit (37 degrees Celsius), is elevated. A low fever is 100°F to 101°F (38°C to 38.5°C). A high fever is 102°F to 104°F (39°C to 40°C). Causes include viruses, bacteria, fungi, drugs, and toxins. Additional symptoms may give an indication of the cause of the fever. If a fever persists, does not respond to analgesics, or goes above 104°F (40°C), you need to seek medical help immediately.

How to Treat a Fever

Have the patient lie down, apply cool wet cloths, remove clothing and blankets until their temperature drops, and give the patient medication to lower their temperature. Ensure that a constant supply of water or fruit juice is taken. Do not feed a patient until the fever has gone, as food may induce vomiting.

51
TREAT SCRAPES AND WOUNDS

Wounds need to be taken seriously in the wild, as they can lead to dangerous blood loss, tissue damage, and infection. Scrapes, even minor ones, especially those incurred by insects or animals, should not be ignored. Even a minor scrape can lead to a serious illness or even death if untreated.

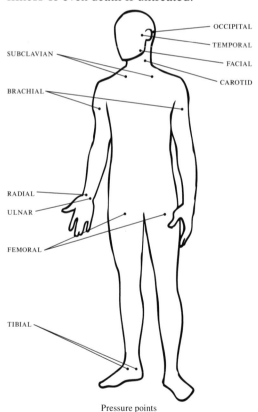

OCCIPITAL

TEMPORAL

SUBCLAVIAN

FACIAL

CAROTID

BRACHIAL

RADIAL

ULNAR

FEMORAL

TIBIAL

Pressure points

SERIOUS BLEEDING

Wounds that occur at pressure points, or where a main artery is close to the surface of the skin, can lead to serious bleeding. You can lose a pint of blood and only suffer slight dizziness, which is not that serious. If you lose more than two pints, you will probably lose consciousness, and if you lose four pints, your heart will probably stop. If the wound is pumping a lot of blood, you must stop the bleeding quickly. Tie a clean bandage or some lint-free material, or place your hand or someone else's hand, over the wound. In five to 15 minutes, the blood should coagulate.

TREAT SCRAPES AND WOUNDS

Assuming that bleeding is not excessive, you should do the following:

- Remove clothing or cut it away from the area.
- Check to make sure there are no other wounds.
- Clean the skin around the wound with warm water and soap, as this will help guard against infection.
- Rinse the wound well with water poured from a height for pressure. This will clean out the wound.

- It is best not to suture the wound completely closed, but instead use butterfly sutures. This will enable any pus from an infection to drain. If you completely wrap the scrape or wound, you will need to check it regularly and, if infection occurs, clean it and leave it uncovered.

INFECTION

Infection of scrapes and wounds is almost inevitable, especially in hot, humid climates where bacteria thrive. Signs of infection include swelling, redness, pain, or a heightened temperature. You may also have pus seeping from the wound or scrape.

To treat an infection, you should have antibacterial cream or a full course of antibiotics in your first aid kit. Take these immediately and complete the course. If you are not well equipped with medicine, you should apply a warm compress to the wound for 30 minutes a few times a day. Remove all bandages and scrape or gently probe the wound with a sterile instrument to remove any pus. Replace with clean bandages and check the wound regularly.

OTHER TREATMENTS

If you are far from civilization and you are concerned about the continual pus seeping out of your wound, there are other options. Try leaving your wound open and allow flies to land on it. Let the maggots clean your wound. Remove them once the wound looks clean. Liquid taken from crushed wild garlic or dock leaves can also be used as a natural antiseptic to clean wounds.

52
COPE WITH EXPOSURE AND HYPOTHERMIA

Hypothermia occurs when the body is unable to maintain a core temperature of at least 95 degrees Fahrenheit (35 degrees Celsius).

Dehydration, lack of food, and fatigue will make you more susceptible to hypothermia. One member of your group may suffer while everyone else remains unaffected. A quick diagnosis is important to enable you to act and warm the victim quickly.

SIGNS OF HYPOTHERMIA

Early signs include:
- Complaints of feeling cold
- Cramps
- Complaints of being tired

This will progress to include:
- Uncontrolled shivering
- Inability to follow simple verbal directions

This will escalate to include:
- Slurring of speech
- Stumbling or falling
- Inability to focus
- Violent behavior

Finally:
- Collapse into coma
- Death (if untreated)

You should be aware that not all sufferers will exhibit all of these symptoms and, depending on the conditions, they may deteriorate very quickly.

TREATMENT

First, you must construct a quick shelter to get the victim out of the wind, rain, and cold. Then, you must remove all their wet clothing and replace with dry clothes or blankets. Give them a warm sugary drink and light a fire if possible. Use your emergency rations and try to increase the victim's blood sugar level.

DO NOT

- Do not give alcohol, as this will actually reduce body temperature.
- Do not rub the patient vigorously, as this will only warm you and not the victim.
- Do not allow others to stand around in the wind and rain as you tend to the patient or you will simply have new patients to treat.
- Do not underestimate the seriousness of the condition. Unless you are treating hypothermia in its very early stages, you need to seek medical help.
- Do not simply tell the sufferer to walk quickly or jump up and down to get warm.

SELF-TREATMENT

If you are alone and find yourself getting cold and shivering, or exhibiting any early signs of hypothermia, act quickly.

Get out of the wind and rain, and take off any wet clothing. Try to get warm. Use all of your emergency rations, especially any high-energy or high-sugar foods. If at all possible, light a fire. Make immediate plans to signal for help using flares, smoke signals, radio, or cell phone.

If you do not stop the progression of hypothermia you may lose consciousness, so act quickly. You will feel tired and lack motivation, but you must stay focused to get warm and call for help while you are still able to function.

53
TREAT SPRAINS, DISLOCATIONS, AND FRACTURES

A sprain occurs when the tissue next to a joint is torn. In a fracture, the bone itself is damaged. Dislocation occurs when the bone is displaced out of the socket. As with all types of injuries, you should always take time to carefully assess the patient's symptoms so that you can give the appropriate treatment. It is advisable, with all suspected injuries, to seek professional medical help quickly.

A HUMBLE SPRAIN

Without medical help or an X-ray, it may be impossible to determine whether someone has simply sprained their wrist or ankle or has sustained a fracture. In either case, the person will suffer pain in the area and some swelling.

To treat these symptoms, you should dip the area in cool water, lightly wrap it with a bandage, and keep it elevated and rested. If you have hurt your ankle and need to get yourself back to civilization, it may not be possible to rest fully. In this case, leave your boot on to act as a support or use a splint in case you have suffered a fracture. Try to lean on a friend, or find a stick to take as much of your weight as possible.

DREADED DISLOCATION

A fully dislocated shoulder, finger, or elbow will be obvious, as the arm or finger will be distorted to the eye. It is best to simply immobilize the area, make sure that blood flow is not compromised, and get professional help.

If you are curious as to how to treat dislocation when stranded with medically untrained friends on a desert island, this is what you might do.

Pull the dislocated finger gently back into place. The thumb is trickier. The shoulder may be treated by putting your clean, unshod foot into the sufferer's armpit and pulling their arm.

Expect some pain, yelling, and unhappiness to follow your treatment. Wrap the area loosely and immobilize it.

FRACTURES

A closed fracture is one where there is no wound or broken skin. An open fracture has an open wound and needs to be treated with potential infection in mind. An open fracture—or one where nerves, ligaments, or organs are damaged or where there is also a dislocation—is considered a complicated fracture.

You will know that you have a fracture if you have heard the faint snap of your bone breaking. However, you may not hear this and still have a fracture.

You will experience pain in the area, which will increase if you try to move. The area will be tender to the touch; swelling and bruising will eventually occur at the site of the fracture. The area may also look deformed. You may hear grinding when you examine the area. It is important to note that not all of these symptoms and signs will be present. If you are in any doubt that the bone is broken, you should treat the area as if there is a fracture.

TREATMENT OF A FRACTURE

If a patient has other injuries, such as difficulty breathing or bleeding, you need to treat those first. Do not move the patient. Unless it is absolutely necessary, treat the fracture at the site of the accident. If this is too dangerous, take some time to immobilize the limb or damaged area before moving. Even supporting the injury with your hand may be sufficient to enable you to move.

Even if there is no open wound, you need to bandage and support the area. Bandages should be tight enough to prevent movement of the area, but not so tight as to limit or prevent circulation. If the patient is going to need to move around, a splint may be necessary to protect the injury.

If the broken limb is making the arm or leg look obviously deformed, you will need to gently apply pressure to straighten the area before splinting and bandaging. This will cause pain to the patient.

OPEN FRACTURE

Never apply pressure to the area of a fracture. If the bone is protruding, you will need to place gauze over the area with care. Then, roll up some bandages or clean strips of cloth into a doughnut shape. Ensure that the center hole is large enough to accommodate the protruding bone. Place this over the injury. Wrap the area lightly with a bandage, wrapping it in a diagonal to avoid applying any direct pressure to the wound.

CIRCULATION

It is important to check all bandages and the splint to make sure that circulation is not compromised. If the area around the bandage appears cold or insensitive to the touch or is discolored, you may need to loosen the bandages. Always elevate the fractured limb, once it has been bandaged and supported, to prevent circulation problems from occurring.

55

AVOID AND TREAT INSECT BITES

INSECT BITES

Insect bites are one of the most common tribulations of outdoor life, especially in the summer months. Fortunately, there are ways to make you seem like a less attractive meal. Developed during World War II for soldiers serving in mosquito-ridden Southeast Asia, DEET remains the original and best military-strength repellent. Applying thin layers of unscented lotion below the repellent will protect your skin and make the DEET last longer. Some research suggests that eating garlic or food containing high levels of B vitamins causes subtle changes in the way your skin smells, rendering your natural odor utterly repulsive to the delicate noses of insects. Wearing light-colored, long-sleeved clothing can also help. As a final solution, a thin layer of wet mud on your exposed skin will form a hard crust as it dries that is impenetrable to most insects. You may look a bit funny, but you'll be the one laughing when your friends become mosquito pincushions while you remain bite-free!

SOME STRATEGIES OF SOOTHING THE ITCHING OF INSECT BITES

For the most part, insect bites are more of an inconvenience than a danger. While that may be relief enough in itself, especially after the other topics discussed here, here are a few tips to help relieve any pesky itching.

Itching is caused by your body's reaction to substances in insect saliva. Removing this saliva from bites soon after they occur, simply by washing the bite site with water or with an alcohol wipe, will knock the characteristic itching on its head before it has a chance to really get going.

Some people find that a change in temperature relieves itching. Try soaking a cloth in really hot or really cold water, or wrapping a cloth around some ice and holding it on the bite. Various items from your basic toiletries set can assuage itching. Simply apply your choice of toothpaste, underarm deodorant, vapor rub, or a wet aspirin to the affected area. Other sources of relief can be found in your food supplies. Gently rubbing the bite with the inside of a banana skin can relieve itching, as can applying some dampened oats. Alternatively, apply an alkaline paste of baking soda and warm water to bites and wash off after a few minutes. Another option is to take the membrane from the inside of an egg and lay it over the bite. As it dries, it will contract, drawing the saliva—and the itchiness—out of the bite. Some people swear by a little bit of honey dabbed onto the bite, but be careful that this doesn't just attract more insects.

Whatever method you choose, be patient. It will heal itself eventually and scratching will make it worse. A final suggestion is over-the-counter bite cream from your nearest pharmacy—but where's the fun in that?

HOW TO TREAT A CATERPILLAR STING

Not all caterpillars are cute and harmless; some are hairy, nasty, and painful. If one of these stings you, stay calm and remove the offending caterpillar from your body. Don't use your bare hands! Use gloves, tweezers, or a trusty stick. Remove all contaminated clothing and wash it in hot water to remove all stray caterpillar hairs. Take some sticky tape, packing tape, or duct tape, and place it over the sting. When you pull it off, you'll pull the little stinging caterpillar hairs out of the skin—as well as some of your own. Repeat several times, using a new piece of tape each time. Wash the area with soap and water, and apply an ice pack if you have one. Apply a little antiseptic cream, or a paste made of baking soda and water, to the sting, and take a painkiller if necessary. As the sting heals, keep an eye out for infections. Taking a photo of the caterpillar, or jotting down a description, might be helpful should you need to go to a doctor, but don't waste time doing this. Needless to say, if you see signs of an allergic reaction, like a swollen face, difficulty breathing, or a quick-spreading rash, seek medical help immediately.

55
TREAT A SNAKEBITE

HOW TO TREAT A SNAKEBITE

No matter how many survival skills you master, in some situations your knowledge just isn't going to be enough. A snakebite is one of them. If you are bitten by a venomous snake, you should go to a hospital as soon as possible. If you don't know whether or not the snake was venomous, you should go to a hospital. The advice in this section is no substitute for professional medical expertise or the appropriate antivenom. That said, there are a number of practical steps you can take to treat yourself before you reach medical care.

VENOMOUS SNAKEBITES

Get away from the snake. Don't waste time and energy, or risk another bite, by trying to catch or kill the snake. Remove clothing and jewelry from the affected area and, if possible, wash the bite with soap and water. Immobilize the bitten area and keep it below the heart. Don't make any incisions to the wound or attempt to suck the venom out of the bite with your mouth. If one is available, a suction device from a commercial snakebite kit can be used to draw venom out of the wound.

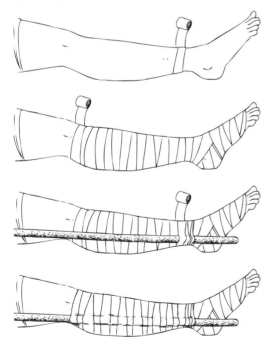

Treating a snakebite

Wrapping a tight crepe or elastic bandage around the bite can reduce blood flow and the speed that the venom spreads. If you don't have a bandage, you can improvise with some stretchy fabric like a T-shirt. Start wrapping about four inches (10 centimeters) away from the fang marks and wrap toward the heart. The bandage should be loose enough to allow a finger to slip under it. Don't use a tourniquet, as this can cut off blood flow completely and may result in the eventual loss of the affected limb. Don't remove the dressing until you reach the hospital. If the bite is on an arm or leg, then splinting the limb will reduce the spread of venom still further.

NONVENOMOUS SNAKEBITES

If you are sure that the snake was nonvenomous, then the only real risk is infection. Clean the wound carefully and apply a thin layer of antibiotic ointment on the bite before bandaging the area to protect the wound as it heals.

AVOID GETTING BITTEN

The best advice of all is to avoid getting bitten. If you come across a snake, simply give it a wide berth and walk around it. A lot of people are bitten because they try to catch, kill, or get a closer look at a snake, succeeding only in annoying it. Don't. It won't be funny when it bites you.

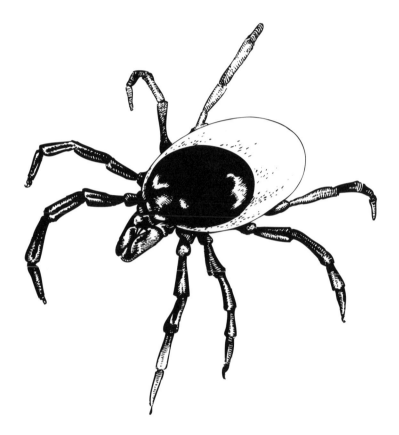

56
REMOVE TICKS

TICKS

Ticks are small, but can be serious; they carry Lyme disease, which can even be fatal. The good news is that you're unlikely to contract Lyme disease unless the tick stays attached for two days or more, which can easily be avoided.

HOW TO REMOVE A TICK

Grasp the head firmly with a pair of tweezers and steadily pull it out. The head is usually buried just beneath your skin, so get your tweezers as close as possible to it. Squeezing the body will cause more of the tick's saliva to be injected in your skin

Deer tick and wood tick size comparison; removing a tick with tweezers

and may leave the head embedded in your skin. As you extract the tick, your skin will probably be pulled up with it until the tick detaches. Treat the wound with an antiseptic or alcohol as soon as possible to help prevent infection. If possible, save the tick in a bag so that your local health department can test it for disease. Always check for more ticks once you have located one.

OTHER METHODS

A pair of tweezers is ideal, but you may not have one handy. It is best to remove the tick quickly and not wait. You can take two credit cards and create makeshift tweezers. You can also use your fingers: thumb and forefinger on the same hand is best. Try not to handle the tick directly and use gloves or plastic bags to cover your hands.

CHECK FOR TICKS

You often don't notice when you're bitten, so it's a good idea to check yourself after you've been in an area where ticks are common. Ticks are usually red or brown and will look like a small bump or scab on your skin. They can be as small as a pinhead, or as large as your fingernail when mature and fully engorged with blood. Common places for ticks to lodge themselves include between fingers and toes, behind knees, behind ears, on the neck, around your hairline and head, and on your stomach and belly button.

LYME DISEASE

Lyme disease does not immediately present itself and can go misdiagnosed and untreated with fatal results. If you have been bitten by a tick, record the event and keep it with your medical records should you develop unusual symptoms related to the tick at a later date.

Stage one will begin either days or weeks after the infection. It is characterized by flulike symptoms and may include itching, chills, fever, headache, muscle pain, fainting, and a stiff neck. You may also develop a "bull's eye" rash, which is a flat or slightly raised rash on the site of the bite. It may grow to 12 inches (30 centimeters) in diameter.

At stage two, the bacteria have been disseminated widely throughout your body. You may suffer from facial paralysis, muscle pain and swelling of joints, and heart palpitations. These symptoms may go and return again. Quick treatment at this stage is essential.

At stage three, you will have muscle and joint pain and may also suffer from weakness, numbness, tingling of muscles, and speech problems.

TREATMENT

If you are bitten by a tick that has been identified as being a potential carrier of Lyme disease, you will be tested or placed on a course of antibiotics. In the early stages, treatment is usually successful and without complications. If you have reached stage three, you may have long-term heart and joint problems. You may also have permanent facial paralysis, vision problems, and memory or sleep disorders.

DO NOT DESPAIR

While it is true that most sufferers of Lyme disease never noticed that they were bitten by a tick, it is also true that most victims of ticks do not ever get Lyme disease. Wear appropriate clothing, use insect repellent, and pack tweezers.

57
AVOID AND DEFEND AGAINST PREDATORS

It is always best to avoid confrontations with predators. Keep away from alligator-infested swamps. Avoid trails with signs of bear activity. Do not cross water in which piranhas live. If a tiger is sighted in the jungle, head quickly in the opposite direction. If there are sharks, do you really need to go for a swim today?

If you only become aware of the predator when you are face-to-face with it, then you will need to consider your options.

MOUNTAIN LIONS
Should you be faced down by a mountain lion, do not run away. You must make loud, threatening noises while stretching out your

arms to make yourself seem big and scary. Crying or failing to retain the contents of your bladder or bowels is not a good idea. If the lion attacks, your only hope is to fight back valiantly and protect your neck from its killer bite.

PIRANHAS

Should you find yourself crossing a piranha-filled lake, you may be OK. Do you have any uncovered cuts in the water? Are the fish already in a feeding frenzy close by? Is it during the day or during a drought? You may want to get out quickly if any of these are true. If, on the other hand, it is nighttime, the water is free flowing, you are uninjured, or you happen to have a bleeding companion walking downstream of you, you will be fine. Simply walk at a slow, steady pace to the far side.

ALLIGATORS

You are facing down a large male alligator more than nine feet (three meters) long and are standing in front of the water. First, try to get out of the way by running really fast. If the alligator lunges and grabs you, hit it hard on the nose to get it to release you. If it manages to drag you into the water, you will probably not make it out again in one piece. Alligators are very difficult to spot, so you should always assume they are around when traveling in their habitat.

STINGING INSECTS

Beset by bees, wasps, or hornets? Run away as fast as you can. Do not stop to check if they are still following you; assume that they are. Get indoors, into a car, or into water. You will then need to remove clothing and bees from your hair, nose, and ears. Seek medical attention, as multiple stings can result in an allergic reaction, even in those not usually prone. It is best to avoid disturbing nests by checking carefully before making camp or lighting fires or torches.

SNAKES

Avoid snakebites by keeping away from long grass and not sticking limbs into dark places. Do not poke snakes or intentionally approach them. They will usually move away from you if you let them. If you find yourself face-to-face with a potentially poisonous snake, move back slowly. A snake will lunge to strike. You will need to be more than five feet (one and a half meters) away from a 10-foot (three-meter) snake to be safe. If you have a stone, club, or forked stick, you may be able to disable the snake, but this will require getting dangerously close to it. If a python wraps itself around you, try to grab its mouth and with your other hand try to unwrap it. Do not wriggle, as this will only increase the pressure it exerts.

CHARGING ANIMALS

If you are faced with a charging animal, try to sidestep out of the way, as many such animals, like the rhinoceros, only charge in straight lines. Other dangerous animals may be evaded once spotted by remaining downwind and not moving. This may be difficult over a long period of time. Most predators in the wild do not consider a human to be prey and will leave the area once they spot you. You want to avoid drawing attention to yourself. If you are spotted, try to leave calmly. Try not to act like a prey animal. Whimpering quietly and sweating profusely in fear may be unavoidable but is not recommended, as most animals have a much keener sense of smell and hearing than humans do.

58
HOW TO RESPOND TO A BEAR ATTACKING

Grizzly bear

WHAT TO DO WHEN
A BEAR ATTACKS

If you are in "bear country," you have to be prepared for a bear encounter. There are bears in every province of Canada, and in all 50 states of the United States. The most common bear in North America is the black bear. Grizzly bears are larger, with humped shoulder muscles. Bears can become accustomed to feeding on garbage and foraging near humans; pay attention to keeping your campsite clean and secure and stay vigilant on the trail. It's helpful to pack bear pepper spray before you set out. This spray creates a cloud that will stop a bear from advancing and allow you to escape an attack.

THE BEAR IS AHEAD

If a bear does not see you and is far from you, steer clear by retreating slowly, downwind if possible. If the bear does see you, retreat slowly, speaking calmly, perhaps to identify yourself as a human. When backing away, avoiding eye contact is advisable—stay aware of the bear.

There are two types of bears to consider: the grizzly bear (large shoulder humps) and the black bear (smaller, no shoulder humps). Grizzly bears do not regard humans as a potential meal and will usually only attack if a hiker surprises them. If you stay alert, you can avoid such an encounter. Black bears may stalk you for their dinner, which will make them harder to escape from unmolested.

THE BEAR SHOWS SIGNS OF AGGRESSION

Again, backing away slowly is the best option. If you know this is a grizzly, you may consider climbing a tree, but many bears can climb trees—grizzly cubs and black bears are especially good at it. You should never run. The bear can run at 30 mph (around 50 kph) on difficult terrain; you cannot. If you run, the bear will consider you to be prey and chase you; a bear will assess the situation, and running will make up the bear's mind.

THE BEAR CHARGES

The bear may perform a "false charge," veering off or stopping at the last moment. Stand your ground. Pepper spray is also an option. Remember, you can't outrun the bear. If the bear stops, backing away slowly will show you are not a threat.

THE BEAR ATTACKS

If the bear attacks you, you can consider fighting, in which case the bear may back down. If you are in daylight, you can "play dead," lying in the fetal position, or more likely on your stomach with your hands clasped behind your neck to protect it. If a bear is attacking you at night, it's more likely that you are being hunted. After an attack, if playing dead has been successful, very carefully assess whether the bear is still in the area, and then retreat, getting assistance as quickly as possible.

BOOK FIVE

WATER

59
FRESHWATER FISH

A freshwater fish is one that can be caught in rivers, streams, ponds, or lakes. Some fish, such as salmon, spend most of their lives at sea but reproduce in fresh water. Some fish are found in a variety of habitats and climates; others are specific to a region. There are too many species to name them all. There are more than 9,000 species in the world, with nearly a thousand in the United States. There are seven different classified orders of freshwater fish. All include some fish that are commonly caught by anglers and are good to eat.

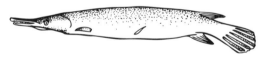

GAR

One of the largest predatory fish is the gar, of which there are five different types. They all have long bodies with diamond-shaped scales and narrow, long snouts. They are predatory fish that can be best found in large, sluggish rivers. The alligator gar can reach up to nine feet (three meters) in length and weigh up to 300 pounds (140 kilograms). They eat fish, and large gar even eat ducks or small mammals. Reportedly, alligator gar tastes more meaty than fishy.

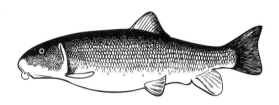

SUCKERS, MINNOWS, AND CARP

A second order of freshwater fish includes suckers, minnows, and carp. These fish can be found in many habitats of the world, and are most numerous and diverse in Southeast Asia.

Sucker fish are easily identifiable by their sucker-shaped mouths, which are usually downturned. They are edible, but are more commonly used as bait or kept in aquariums, as they do not grow very large. They are native to nearly all the Great Lakes of the United States and are also found in Central and South America.

Minnows can be found in almost all freshwater habitats in the United States, Asia, and Europe. They are commonly used as bait, but can be eaten. There are more than 2,000 identified species. Common characteristics include one dorsal fin with only nine rays and a small abdominal pelvic fin, with all fins being soft and flexible. These are long and moderately thick fish.

Carp can be found on every continent except South America. They can live for more than 30 years, and the common carp can grow to nearly four feet (more than a meter) long. They can be very difficult to catch. Some anglers recommend pouring canned corn into the river to draw them out.

CATFISH

Catfish are distinctive and easily recognizable, as they have no scales and a slightly downturned mouth with eight barbels sticking out of it. They are edible, but many people recommend no longer eating them due to the high mercury levels found in the fish.

PIKE

Fish of the order that includes pike are very popular with anglers and are found in fresh water throughout the Northern Hemisphere. They are predators, grow quite large, can be difficult to catch, and are perfectly edible. They are not known for their taste, but for the sport in catching them. The largest pike ever caught was five feet (one and a half meters) long and weighed more than 55 pounds (25 kilograms).

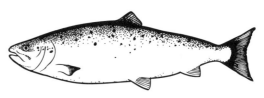

SALMON AND TROUT

Salmon and trout are popular with anglers due to their palatable taste, and are found in clean, clear rivers, streams, and lakes. They are native to North America, Asia, and Europe and have been introduced to Australia and New Zealand. Those species returning from the ocean may look quite silvery in color, but with time they get more vivid colors, depending on the habitat, the longer they live in fresh water. They have small scales on the body, no scales on the head, and no spines on their fins.

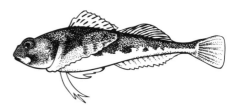

SCULPINS

Fish in the sculpin group have large mouths and heads, few or no scales, and large pectoral fins. They are predatory fish, mainly eating insects, and tend to lie on the riverbed. These fish are also found in salt water, but are mainly found in the Northern Hemisphere in fresh water. Some species grow to two feet (60 centimeters) long. They are edible, but are not considered to be tasty.

BASSES AND SIMILAR SPECIES

The last order includes temperate basses, sunfish, perches, and drums. This group forms the largest order of all vertebrates in the world, with nearly 10,000 species, most of which are marine fish.

The temperate basses are native to North America, Europe, and North Africa. They have forked tails, and are silvery with dark horizontal stripes, large mouths, and two dorsal fins. They can be up to 50 pounds (23 kilograms) in weight. They are predatory, live in schools, and are easier to spot hunting at dusk close to the water's surface. They are edible and will put up a good fight when you try to catch them.

Sunfish are popular, as the smaller varieties can be very good to eat. They have between six and 13 dorsal spines, a soft dorsal fin, and a rounded or forked tail fin. During breeding season, male sunfish can be brightly colored. They can be found in quiet, slow-moving rivers and streams. They naturally occur in the United States and have been introduced in Africa, Asia, and Europe.

Perch are common in Europe and in America, Asia, and Australia. The European perch is the most widely found and caught type. They are green with a light red or orange coloring to the tips of their fins. They usually weigh around one pound (500 grams); they can be caught using almost any type of bait quite easily and are considered good to eat.

Saltwater drum fish can be found in North and Central America. They grow to 40 pounds (18 kilograms) in weight, and are silvery in color with a humped back. They are carnivorous fish. While larger specimens may be challenging to catch, they are edible. They need to be eaten very fresh, as they dry out and lose flavor quickly.

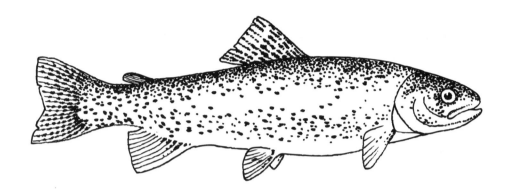

60
CATCH AND COOK A TROUT

To catch a trout using the bait and lure fishing method, you will need the following: a fishing rod, a reel, a hook, a line, and weights. These can be purchased from a sporting goods or fishing shop or borrowed from kindly neighbors or relatives. You may need a fishing license or permit. You will need a suitable river or lake that is naturally or artificially stocked with trout. You will also need bait. A net and a bucket will also be useful.

ROD
Your rod should be rated for two- to eight-pound (one- to three-and-a-half-kilogram) fish. You will need four- to eight-pound (two- to three-and-a-half-kilogram) rated fishing line. You should have number 6 to number 10 hooks, and some weights that you can hook to your line. Adding a weight will allow you to cast more accurately and will also allow you to control the drift of your bait. Weights should ideally be placed about two feet (60 centimeters) above the hook on your line.

BAIT
If you are using bait, there may be restrictions in the river you fish as to the type. Common types used for trout include live earthworms from your garden, salmon

roe, and canned corn. Artificial lures may be added to attract the fish. The faster the river, the heavier the lure should be. Change your bait depending on the weather. Fish will likely be attracted to earthworms after heavy rain, while lures mimicking insects may attract them on windy days.

CASTING FOR TROUT

Trout like to swim facing upstream to catch food drifting toward them. Look at the river. If you spot trout, go downstream of them and cast upstream. Your bait and lure will then drift toward them in a lifelike manner.

Face the river and cast your line upstream. To cast your line, bring the rod up so that it is slightly behind you and then quickly bring the rod tip forward while releasing the line. If you have a button reel, simply move your thumb off the button. If you are holding the line with your forefinger, release your hold until the line hits the water.

Now, wait for the current to bring the line past you. Continually reel in the line to ensure that it remains taut. Keep holding the rod with the tip up at the level of your face.

If there is no bite on the line, slowly reel in, check your bait, and cast off again.

CATCHING A FISH

If the tip of your rod dips sharply, you may have hooked a fish. You need to quickly lift the rod tip up by at least one foot (30 centimeters). If the fish is caught, it will bend the rod. Reel in your fish. Do not lower the tip of the rod, as this will enable the trout to get away. Once the fish is close enough to reach, use your net.

TOP TIPS

The best time to fish for trout is at dusk or dawn. If you head out in the midday sun, you will not catch anything.

If you are able to see a trout in the water, the trout is able to see you. Stay well back from the edge of the water—or, even better, sit down—to avoid scaring away the fish. Shouting and jumping next to the river will also scare away the fish.

If you get your line caught in nearby trees, shrubs, or weeds, do not pull it sharply from far away. It could come loose and end up hooked to your face. Move to where it is caught and cut it loose. If you want to retrieve your hook, you can free it by pulling it in varying directions. The hook is liable to come away and fly directly toward you. It is a good idea to wear glasses and a hat, as this will at least prevent hooks from entering your eyes.

COOK A TROUT

If you have caught a small one- or two-ounce (30–60-gram) brown trout, you can eat it whole. Simply make a small slice in the belly and scoop the innards out with your finger. Fry the fish in butter for a minute or so and then pop into your mouth. It will taste delicious and sweet.

If you have a slightly larger trout, it is still very simple to prepare and cook. Slice the belly open from tail to head and gut the fish, disposing of the digestive tract and guts. Now, simply take the head off by cutting in a V-shape and take off the pectoral fins as well. Rinse your fish in cold water. You can fry, barbecue, or bake trout in a little butter.

If you wish to fillet your trout, gut and remove its head and fins. Then, place the trout stomach-up on your table and cut up and down along the backbone from head to tail. You will clearly see the rib cage, which you can remove by cutting under it. Take the backbone away from the tail with your knife and pull it away gently. Use your hands to take out the bones from the fillets of the fish. This is called butterflying your trout.

Baked trout is a high-protein, low-fat meal. Simply coat the prepared fish with oil and your chosen herb or spice and cook in a medium oven for about 20 minutes.

You can experiment by basting the fish with lemon and herbs and butter. Get a large piece of tinfoil, roughly three times the width of the fish. Wrap the fish so that there is room around it, but the tinfoil is pinch-sealed all around. Place in an oven for about 15 minutes.

To cook your trout over your campfire, coat it in oil or butter, place it on a grill, and cook for 12 minutes, turning once. Flip it over carefully, as it will break apart if handled roughly. If you have filleted your trout, it will only take about eight minutes to cook.

It is best to either freeze your trout immediately or, if cooking fresh trout, eat it within one or two days of catching it.

Do not remove the scales of the trout.

Do not overcook your trout.

61
HOW TO BUILD A RAFT

In this section, you will learn how make a basic "Man-Friday" raft, a dry deck, and anchors.

GETTING STARTED

Before you begin constructing your raft, you will need to gather the appropriate pieces of wood. A hammer and saw would be useful, but you can manage if you have a good knife or axe for sizing and fashioning the wood and some stones for banging the pegs into place.

First, select two pine logs of equal length to form the sides of the raft, and two long saplings that you can use for braces. You will also need three shorter logs of roughly the same length to form the crosspieces of the raft. Select the heaviest one to be the bow. Bore a hole near each end of the crosspieces, which will later be used to affix them to the frame. For guidance, see B, C, and D in Fig. 1.

Finally, you will need to fashion 10 pegs, with a groove down one side, which will be used to fasten the pieces of wood together.

To create the main base of the raft, sharpen the butt (larger end) of the two long logs on one side with the axe, making a chisel edge as shown in Fig. 1. Place the saplings across them diagonally, trim them to the right length, and nail them into position, as in the diagram. You have now completed the raft's basic frame.

CONTINUING CONSTRUCTION

Bear in mind that the finished raft will be very heavy and difficult to lift. Because of this, it is more sensible in the long run to continue construction in the water, even though raft-building would be much more easily executed on land. So take off your socks and shoes and roll up your pants, take all of your logs in the water, and secure them in a shallow spot.

ATTACHING THE CROSSPIECES

Attaching the crosspieces will give the raft enough strength to support a man's weight. For this stage, you will only need the two lighter crosspieces—you will attach the bow later. First, lay the two crosspieces in position on top of the raft frame and carefully mark the logs through the holes. These marks will allow you to see exactly where you will need to attach the crosspieces.

Take one log first and, using these marks as guides, bore holes in the log that are deep

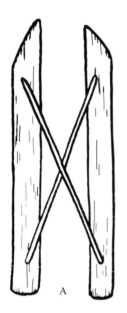

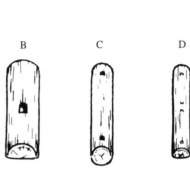

Fig. 1—Parts of the sailing raft

A—Logs in place with braces; B, C, and D—Struts;
E—Raft with middle and stern strut in place.

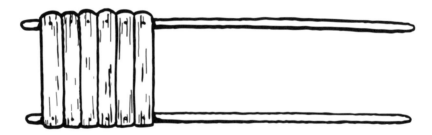

Fig. 2—Dry deck

Fig. 3—Dry deck in place

enough to hold one of your pegs. Fill the holes with water.

Once you have done this, hold a crosspiece in place over this log, take a peg, and drive it through the holes deep into the log. Repeat this process for the other crosspiece.

The water will cause the peg to swell and tighten its hold on the log and crosspieces, while the grooves in the pegs will allow excess water to escape.

To complete this stage, repeat the steps on the other log: bore holes under those in the crosspieces, fill them with water, and finally drive the pegs home just as you did on the first log. Fig. 1, example E, is what you are aiming for; this is the "Man-Friday" raft.

THE DRY DECK

If you want to make a really impressive raft, then you will also need a dry deck. A dry deck not only looks good, it is also practical; it gives you somewhere dry to sit while you use your raft. You can see a picture of the finished product in Fig. 3.

For the dry deck, you will need more wood, so secure your raft in shallow water and go ashore. Find two long elastic ash or hickory poles, which will form the springs. Trim the ends off flat on one side and role the poles over so the flat side is toward the ground. For the deck proper, you will need some reasonably flat wood, like planks or barrel staves. Failing that, split a number of small logs in half. Arrange them close together at one end of the springs to create a rectangular seat, as in Fig. 2, and peg or nail them in place.

Carry the assembled deck down to the raft and place it in position. The flattened sides of the springs should rest on top of the logs at the bow (front) and the seat should be raised up over the middle crosspiece and positioned toward the stern (rear) of the raft.

Bore holes through the springs into the logs at the bow and into the crosspiece in the center of the craft. Fill the holes with water and peg it all together, just as you did before. Finally, place the heavy bow crosspiece over the flat ends, and fasten it in position (Fig. 3).

At this point, you will have before you a fully functional raft, suitable for traveling, fishing, and all manner of waterborne adventures. To really complete the job, there is just one more thing you need—anchors.

THE ANCHORS

Every boat needs anchors to keep it safe, and your raft is no exception. How would you like to see your handiwork floating away for want of an hour's work? I thought not.

The type of anchor you're going to make is called the "keelig." This anchor is all the rage among fishermen off the coast of New

England. It takes very little time to make, and you only need a forked stick, a stone, and a piece of plank or a barrel stave. You will need two anchors: one for the bow and one for the stern.

To secure your lines to the "keelig," take the end of the rope in your right hand and the standing part (which is the part leading from the boat) in your left hand to form a loop.

With your anchors in place, you really have finished. Well-done and happy rafting!

62
TRAVEL ON A RIVER

Traveling on a river can be both a pleasant and fast way to get to your destination. You do need to avoid obstructions in the water, ensure you stay afloat, and, of course, have a contingency plan should everything go horribly wrong.

CURRENT AND OBSTRUCTIONS

Even if you are traveling on a well-built raft that is not overloaded, you cannot afford to sit back and enjoy the scenery. Someone must remain on the lookout for changes in the current, dangerous waters ahead, or signs of rocks or obstacles in the water. You should check the depth of the water and the speed of the current when you set out. Throw a stick in the water to see how fast it moves. Wide, deep rivers tend to be slower than narrow, shallow ones. If the river is moving faster than you can swim and your raft is not very robust, you should consider another form of transport.

Once you are traveling, look ahead to watch how the water is moving. If you notice water spray or mist ahead, move your raft to the bank, as there may be fast-moving water with obstructions, rapids, or a waterfall ahead.

If you notice changes in the surface movement of the water, such as localized wave patterns or swirling water, avoid this area. There may simply be weeds there, but there could also be submerged rocks or other obstacles that could damage or capsize your raft.

PREDATORS

While you are watching out for rocks and waterfalls, you should also watch out for alligators, crocodiles, or any other large predators or animals that may inhabit the water or riverbank.

IN A CRISIS

If at any time you consider the current or speed of the river to have changed and become unsafe, make for shore immediately and continue on foot.

If you do not notice oncoming rocks or rapids, some earlier preparations can be beneficial. No one should have a heavy pack tied to them. Safety lines can be used to secure each person to the raft if you are in a survival situation. It is preferable for each passenger to have a life jacket.

If you are knocked into the water due to the raft capsizing, try not to panic and flail around. If the water is moving fast, it is unlikely that you will be able to catch the raft and it is safer to make for the riverbank. You can then signal to other members of your party, if they have not noticed your hasty departure, to pull over to the bank and you can walk up to them. If you were tethered to the raft, they can simply pull you aboard. It is safer to use a stick or rope to pull someone aboard. Always catch them under their arms and direct them to lift their leg onto the side. Before you help someone climb aboard, ensure that another person is there or that you are tied to the raft to prevent being pulled in.

If you find yourself in the water with rocks, try to twist your body so that you can push off the oncoming rock with your feet. If you are pushed under and lose your sense of direction, allow yourself to sink so that you can push up from the riverbed with your feet. Make for dry land quickly.

AT NIGHT

It is not safe to travel on a river at night. You need to drag your raft up on the bank, tie it securely, and make a camp in a nearby spot at a safe distance from the river.

CROSSING A RIVER

Should you need to cross a river by foot, the general safety rule is this: If the river is moving moderately fast and is above your knee, you should find another way. If you still wish to cross, consider sending a tall, fit person over first without their backpack. They can carry a rope to the other side, which, if tied to both sides, can be used as a safety line. Do not tie yourself to the rope or to each other. It is safest to unclip your pack so that you can dump it quickly if you are swept under the water.

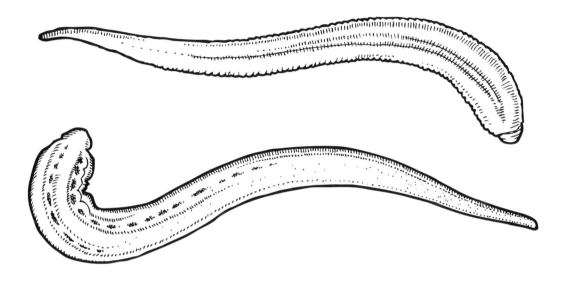

63
REMOVE LEECHES FROM THE BODY

WHAT ARE LEECHES?

Leeches are predatory parasitic segmented worms that are related to the earthworm. They have 32 brains and up to three sets of eyes. They mostly live in water, both salt and fresh, although some live in moist, warm soil. Leeches can be found clinging to plants, on rocks, on animals, or, less fortunately, on your skin. They can be anywhere from two to 10 inches (five to 25 centimeters) long and are found in every continent of the world except Antarctica. When they attach to your skin, they feed voraciously. Five large leeches can drain a small animal of all its blood in half an hour. The best policy is to avoid letting them attach in the first place. If this plan is unsuccessful, do not panic. There is both a right and wrong way to remove a leech.

AVOIDING LEECHES ATTACHING TO YOUR SKIN

As prevention is the best cure, taking the following precautions before hiking in leech-infested areas may prove useful:

- Wear long pants and tuck them into socks.
- Do not wear sandals; wear closed shoes.
- Spray insect repellent in clothes and shoes.
- Rub detergent soap into pants and socks before embarking.
- Put tobacco in your socks, as this has been known to repel leeches.

WHAT NOT TO DO

Do not attempt any of the commonly used techniques of burning off the leech, pouring salt on the leech, or squeezing the leech. All of the above will result in the leech vomiting harmful bacteria into your open wound. This can lead to infection.

LEAVE THE LEECH ON

If you are a particularly brave, intrepid explorer, leaving the leech on to continue feeding is actually the best policy. Even if the leech is large, the loss of blood will not be significant to a human. It will fall off naturally when it is full after about 20 minutes. The leech bite will not hurt, as it injects a small amount of anaesthetic. When it falls off, simply apply some antiseptic cream and continue on hiking. As you cannot feel leeches attach, it is a good policy upon finding a leech to thoroughly check for others, and for all members of your party to check for leeches as well.

TAKING THE LEECH OFF

If, like most people, you find leeches repellent, and the idea of one continuing to ingest your blood as you hike disturbing, the following is a quick guide to removing one safely.

Locate the narrow end of the leech; this will be where its head and sucker are. Slide a sharp object or your fingernail under the sucker. Move quickly to remove the sucker off your skin to prevent the leech from vomiting back the blood into your wound. Flick the leech away to prevent it from reattaching to your skin. Clean the wound with soap and bandage it. It will bleed due to the anticlotting enzymes in the leech's mouth. Should you experience a rash, dizziness, or sweating, it may simply be an allergic reaction to the bite; you should take antihistamines and seek medical attention when possible.

LEECHES IN YOUR MOUTH

Should you be unfortunate enough to get a leech inside of your mouth while swimming, you will be eager to remove it quickly. Gargling with the strongest alcoholic drink in your supply kit will be necessary to dislodge your unwelcome visitor. Inclusion of a small bottle of strong alcohol in your kit should be considered if you intend to swim in any swamps.

64
SURVIVE ON OR NEAR A BEACH OR ISLAND

Shorelines can provide ample foraging and hunting grounds and materials for fires and shelters. It is preferable to make for a beach or island rather than to remain aboard a raft. It will be easier to signal for rescue and easier to survive.

HAZARDS

As with any survival situation, there will be hazards and challenges specific to surviving on a beach or island. For example, you risk being cut by coral or sharp rocks when fishing or foraging. If you are cut by coral, do not treat the wound with iodine, as some coral feed on this. Always wash all cuts and grazes thoroughly, as the risk of contracting an infection is one of the major obstacles to survival.

There will be wildlife to contend with. Many dangerous animals—such as saltwater crocodiles, stingrays, venomous snakes, eels, and fish with poisonous and sometimes deadly stings—could be encountered. Warm, tropical waters will hold more hazards than colder or more temperate seas.

Tides and undertow will also present a hazard. It may not be possible to avoid entering the water. You should use extreme caution, watch where you place your feet, and, preferably, tie yourself to an anchor line on the shore.

WATER

If you find yourself on an isolated shore or a small island, you may have difficulty finding a source of fresh water. Finding or collecting water should always be your first priority, unless extreme weather necessitates immediate shelter.

It is possible to find fresh water by searching above the high tide line. Cracks in rocks may hold fresh rainwater. Greenery is usually a good indicator of where to look. You may need to move inland to find water, although this may not be ideal for rescue purposes. If you cannot find any springs or convenient picturesque waterfalls nearby, you may need to set up water collection devices. Water will collect as condensation in bags tied over plants, especially in climates with a high variation in temperature between day and night. It is also a good idea to tie up containers, as many as possible, to collect rainwater. This is safe to drink without boiling if the container is clean and it is not left to sit. It is also possible to create a water still to purify salt water for drinking. This will require a lot of fuel, is time consuming, and will only produce a small amount of water. Use this method only in conjunction with other water-procurement techniques.

SHELTER

Use any and all available materials to make a shelter to protect against wind, rain, sun, and cold. If you have a raft, lean it up against a rock or trees as an immediate shelter. You can then forage and collect materials for a more suitable structure at your leisure. All debris you collect on the beach or from your wreckage can be employed. Take care that you build your shelter above the high tide line. Look for a change in the color of sand, greenery, a line of seaweed, or an end to debris thrown up by the sea as indicators of the high tide line. If you are in a tropical location or the weather is stormy, move back farther from the shoreline.

Ideally, you want your shelter to be close enough to the shore to spot passing vessels. If you find a good fresh source of water, you will want your shelter to be close to this, too.

Avoid building a shelter in sand dunes. They may offer protection from the wind, but you will be plagued by insects.

FOOD

There are many sources of food available on the seashore to forage and hunt. You need to use caution, however, as not all available food is safe to eat. Many fish are poisonous to humans. There are about 1,200 species of venomous fish. They include stonefish, lionfish, scorpion fish, and toadfish. They will not be rendered safe by cooking or by using any other method. There will be no indication either in the smell or taste of the fish, and birds may eat them safely. Once you eat a poisonous fish, you may suffer numbness, itching, nausea, vomiting, or death. Some poisonous fish can induce hallucinations if eaten. These include the *Sarpa salpa* of the Mediterranean and the *Siganus spinus* found off the coast of Hawaii.

Once you are clear about the safe species to eat, fish will provide you with a nutritious meal. Their eyes and spines contain fresh water, and their bones may be used as camp needles. Shellfish and mollusks are easy to procure without fishing equipment and are a good source of protein. Happily feast on mussels, limpets, or clams. Sea slugs can also be cooked and eaten. Wear gloves when catching crabs or lobsters to avoid an injury.

For variety in your menu, do not ignore your greens. Seaweed can be cooked and eaten like spinach if it is fresh and wet. If it is dry or smells, use it only as fuel for your fire. Not all species are edible, so clearly identify it first. There are also edible varieties of sea urchins. Do not attempt to harvest these with your hands, as their sharp spines give a painful sting.

An island may produce other food sources if you travel to hunt and forage a little inland. You may find fruit, coconuts, or eggs, and birds and small mammals may be trapped and hunted.

RESCUE

Once you have secured your water, built your shelter, and eaten your dinner, you may start to consider rescue. It is better to remain close to the shore. If you are unsure of your location, traveling inland is not a good idea. If you need to travel, go up or down the coast unless an inland trail gives a clear indication of human habitation. Light a campfire and collect as much fuel for your fire as possible. Have a ready supply of damp grass, leaves, moss, or rubber next to your fire to create smoke and alert passing vessels. If possible, create a fire on high ground. Place debris or rocks in an SOS pattern or another unnatural way to be spotted from the air close to the shore. Make yourself as visible as possible.

65
DISTILL SALT WATER

SALT WATER

You should never drink salt water unless it is distilled. The body will need to secrete more water through urinating to rid itself effectively of the extra saline. Drinking salt water will dehydrate you faster than not drinking at all. Humans cannot survive on salt water, although some have claimed that in extreme situations drinking two cups of salt water and three cups of fresh water per day can be sustained with no ill effects.

FUEL CONSUMPTION

Distilling water consumes large amounts of fuel. It is estimated that it takes one gallon (four liters) of fuel to produce one gallon of water.

HOW IT WORKS

A still is a means of purifying salt water, or any water with known contaminants. Urine may also be distilled in this way. It works by heating the salt water to create steam, and then collecting the steam and allowing it to condense into drinkable water. A solar still works on the same principle, but creates condensation using the heat of the sun.

SOLAR STILL

It is possible to construct a solar still that requires no fire. To make one, dig a hole, pour salt water inside, place a clean container in the middle of the hole, cover the hole with plastic, seal down the plastic, and place a stone on top of the plastic to weigh it down over your container. The salt water will evaporate in the heat and drip back into your glass.

This will only work if the soil in which you place the still is hot and damp from the sun and the plastic is cold. A solar still will only produce one pint (500 milliliters) of water in any 24-hour period. It can be useful as a supplement to other water-collection methods. It is best to run a tube from the freshly produced water so you can sip from it as it collects instead of disturbing the still or waiting for a whole day. It is not possible to survive with water retrieved from a solar still alone.

CONSTRUCT YOUR STILL

If you are very organized, you may have a distilling flask among your supplies. This has two sections: the lower section holds the salt water, and the higher section carries the freshly condensed water. Simply fill it with salt water and leave it in the sun, or place it over the fire. Empty the fresh water and refill the salt water as necessary. If you have a glass distilling flask, place it over a flame and collect the water as it drips out. A common distilling flask, which you may recognize from science class in school, can be filled with salt water and suspended over your fire, waiting to collect fresh water as it drips out. You are unlikely to have such a flask lying around.

Are you not that organized? Do not fret. You will need two containers, one length of tubing, a fire, and plenty of firewood. First, fill one pot with salt water and put it over the fire to boil. Cover it well and run a piece of tubing from this pot into your collection pot nearby. Cover this pot. Try to seal both pots so that all the steam gets forced into the tube and drips into the collection pot. Use wet sand or strips of material to achieve this. The more steam you keep from escaping, the higher your yield of fresh water. Your collection pot needs to be cold. Set it in salt water or in the shade, or partially bury it in damp soil.

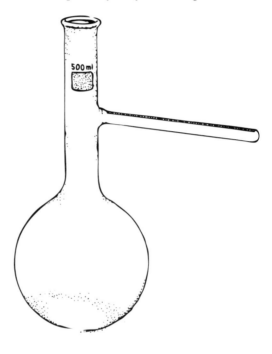

66
FORAGE ON THE BEACH

The beach will yield a wide variety of food if you know where to look and are open-minded about your menu plan.

SEAWEED

There are many edible varieties of seaweed. You can retrieve them from pools or the sea. If they are alive and floating and do not have any blue algae present, they are usually safe to eat.

One of the most popular types is sea lettuce, usually found where streams run into the sea; this has light green leaves. Wash the leaves and cook by boiling for a short time in water.

Kelp is common in the Atlantic and Pacific on rocky seashores. It is rich in carotene, iodine, and chromium. Kelp has a cylindrical stalk and long, thin leaves that can be olive green or dark brown. You can eat kelp raw, but it tastes better boiled lightly like spinach. While all types of seaweed are edible, some have a laxative effect, while others may induce vomiting. Consult your guide to plants that are safe to eat, which you carefully packed, before ingesting seaweed. Alternatively, you can get a member of your party to volunteer to test the seaweed. If they have not run screaming to the camp latrine after five hours, then you can add the seaweed to your menu plan.

MOLLUSKS AND CRUSTACEANS

When foraging on the beach, search in all the rock pools at low tide. It may be possible to find crabs or lobsters, although gloves and a net will be necessary to retrieve them without incurring an injury. Even if you are not that lucky, you can still provide yourself with much-needed protein. Limpets, bashed off of rocks, can be placed, in their shells, on rocks next to your fire and roasted. Once they are golden brown, remove the shell and guts and chew vigorously. You may also place these in your rock pool seafood chowder.

You can also eat clams, mussels, barnacles, periwinkles, and some sea urchins. It is best to leave all mollusks in their shells and place them in a pot with your seaweed to boil for at least five minutes. With clams and mussels, ensure that the shell is tightly shut or else discard it. Periwinkles should close their valves if you bang them. Limpets should not be easy to remove from a rock; this means they are fresh and safe to eat. Avoid mussels in the tropics in the summer and black mussels in the Arctic at any time of the year.

SEABIRDS AND NESTS

If seabirds occupy the shore, consider trapping them. Put out bait on a line with a barbed hook that will stick in the bird's mouth to catch it. If you are on a beach and notice nesting birds, consider raiding the nests for eggs. Seabirds may attack you if they see you too close to their nests, so be ready to steal the eggs and escape from the unhappy parents.

WORMS

Worms on the beach can be used as bait for fishing. Look for marks in the sand and dig for worms. Sea snails, found in rock pools, can be eaten like any other mollusk.

INSECTS

If you are very open-minded, consider catching and eating insects, which may be abundant in sand dunes. Avoid flies or insects that feed on carrion. Make sure that you cook any beetles, as insects with shells usually carry parasites. Enjoy your meal. Remember that insects are low in fat and high in protein.

67
FISH FROM THE SEASHORE

In order to fish from the shore, you will need certain equipment. It may be possible, if stranded unexpectedly in the wilderness, to use or make substitutes.

EQUIPMENT

You want a suitable rod and reel for sea fishing. If you are fishing for medium-size fish, use a 15-pound (seven-kilogram) line. This will be easy to cast a good distance. You will need to change to a 25-pound (11-kilogram) line for really large fish.

You will need weights, floats, and hooks. Always purchase two of everything for your fishing kit. If you are fishing in calm water with no strong tides, you can use a two-ounce (50-gram) weight on your line. If the sea is rough or there are rocks nearby, use a heavier four-ounce (100-gram) weight.

You do not need a large hook to catch a large fish. If you use a larger hook, you will avoid catching smaller fish. The length of the hook you use should match the bait you are using. If you are using ragworms, you will want a longer hook on which to thread them.

You will also want to bring a knife, a bucket, and a first aid kit with Band-Aids, sterile dressings, and something to clean any cuts.

BAIT

The type of bait you use depends on what fish you are trying to catch and whether you plan to float fish or bottom fish.

If you are a beginner, use mackerel strips on a small, short hook to catch mackerel. You can then freeze your own mackerel to have bait available for future fishing expeditions.

Other baits that you can use for float fishing include ragworms, sand eels, and squid.

If you are using heavy weights and are bottom fishing, use ragworms, crabs, or squid.

Ragworms are popular with all fish, but are prone to fall off the line or be eaten by smaller fish. To avoid this, add more than one worm to your hook and put on some mackerel or strips of eel as well. This will prevent the worm from falling off the hook and should ensure there is enough bait to attract larger fish.

FISHING TIPS

If you are not catching any fish, change your location, depth, or bait.

You may not be setting your float at the correct depth. Mackerel usually stay around six to 10 feet (two to three meters) under the water and garfish swim between eight to 18 feet (two and a half to five and a half meters) under the water. Cast and set your depth, by attaching weights and floats, to about 10 feet (three meters). If after 10 minutes you have not had any action, add more floats or weights.

If others are catching fish near you and you are not, you may be doing something wrong. Ask them how deep they are fishing and what bait they are using and copy them.

After 30 minutes, your bait will no longer be leaving a scent trail in the water and will need to be changed.

Adding beads and shiny material to your line can attract fish.

If you have not had a bite, reel in your line slowly, as you may attract a fish while doing so.

If you are bottom fishing—that is, weighting your line so that the hook rests near the seabed—throw some bait down where you plan to cast. This will create a good scent trail and attract fish to the area.

Small fish you plan to throw back or any bait can be used for this. This will only work if the water is relatively calm. Other people fishing nearby will not appreciate you trying to hog all the fish, so do this discreetly.

SAFETY

When fishing alone from the seashore, rocks, cliff, or pier, consider your own safety. Wearing a flotation suit or life jacket will prevent you from drowning, and will also protect you from shock should you fall into cold water. A whistle tied to your clothes will help you call for help should you get swept out to sea and there are other people fishing from the shore. Let others know where you will be and when you will be back, and only plan a short fishing trip if you are alone. Bring a cell phone in a plastic bag so that you are contactable. If you do not return on time and do not answer your phone, your friends will know you are in trouble.

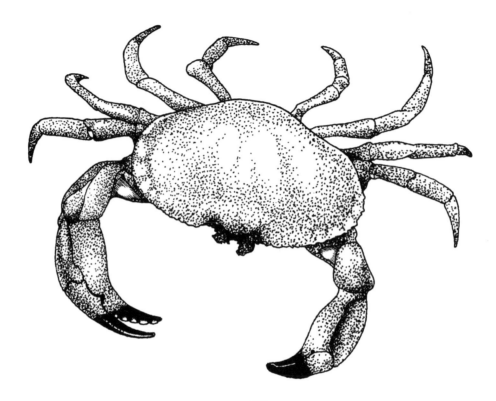

68

CATCH AND COOK CRUSTACEANS

It is possible to catch a crab or a lobster with only a small amount of knowledge, equipment, and patience.

TO CATCH A CRAB

You will need some line; it does not have to be fishing line—it can be string. Crabs are greedy and will ignore the line, even when you are pulling it, once you use bait.

Simply tie any raw meat to your line. You can use limpets bashed off of a nearby rock and fixed on a hook, or fish heads from an earlier catch.

You will also need a net and a small stick. You can improvise a net by bending a thin stick into a hoop and covering it with material, such as a spare T-shirt. It is a good idea to have a bucket or small filled rock pool nearby that you can cover to keep your crab alive and fresh until you are ready to gut it and cook it. Gloves or some makeshift protection for your hands are also needed for crab or lobster fishing.

FIND YOUR SPOT

Crabs can be found in tidal rock pools, or near cliff rocks or harbor walls. You need to go out to find crabs at low tide or as the tide is turning. They will remain hidden until coaxed out with bait. Tie your line to your stick and tie your fish head to the end of your line. Place the bait in a seaweed-free area of the rock pool and wait. Once the crab gets a good hold of the bait, raise the line very slowly and net the crab quickly. It will be possible to reuse the bait, although you may need to move and check out adjacent rock pools periodically.

An alternative method is to throw crushed limpets into the rock pool and use the net to scoop up the investigating crabs, or grab the crabs with your gloved hand.

STORAGE

You can place crabs in a bucket with a small amount of water or in a container with damp seaweed. Make sure the crab cannot climb out, but do not deprive it of air. It is best to eat crabs on the day you catch them. Never attempt to cook or eat a crab you find dead.

LOBSTER

If you fancy catching a lobster, you will need gloves, a stick, a bag, and a net. You can find lobsters in shallow water, or in reefs and rock pools. When you are searching for lobsters, look in cracks and ledges. You will find them in groups, so once you spot one you have a good chance of catching more than one. You will usually spot their antennae or one of their legs poking out of the water.

Approach the lobster slowly. Lower your net in front of the lobster and then leave it immobile so that the creature stops noticing it. Wait a moment or two. Then, using your stick, gently prod the lobster so that it walks onto the net. Raise the net and pop the lobster into your waiting bag.

Lobsters you catch should be longer than three inches (eight centimeters) and should not have any eggs. Catching larger male lobsters ensures that you do not deplete the population in the area.

COOK A CRAB

The heavier the crab, the more meat it will produce. First, place a pot of salted water over your fire until it is boiling. Drop your live crab into the water. If it weighs less than two pounds (one kilogram), 15 minutes will be enough cooking time. If you are cooking more than one crab, ensure that the water has returned to a rolling boil before you add each crab to the pot.

Remove the crab from the pot and allow it to cool. Pull off the crab's claws and legs and lay it on its back facing away from you. Push up under the rear edge of the shell so that the meaty core comes away from the shell. Use your thumbs to dig out the inedible eyes, mouth, digestive tract, and other inedible parts at the front and discard. Also discard the gray-looking gills at the side of the core meat, as they are unpleasant tasting. Now, fish out all the nice meat from the core, discarding any rigid bony pieces, until you have a pile of shredded white crabmeat. Use a knife or stone to crack the claws and remove the meat. Place all the meat in a bowl. Mash the crabmeat into a paste, adding lemon juice and pepper or other herbs and spices that you have and like. You can now clean out the crab shell and use it as a dish for your crabmeat meal.

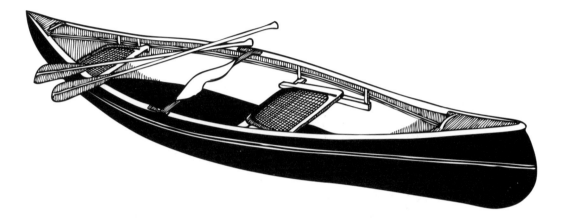

69
MAKE A CANOE

Canoes have been made in the wild, using very few tools, for millennia. These days you have a choice. You can spend a weekend going to your local timber merchant and fashioning a plywood version, or you can spend a month fashioning a canoe like a Native American from the trunk of a tree. You can also make a canoe using birchbark, fiberglass, or canvas.

PLYWOOD CANOE

As with any building project, taking your time and getting some help from a handy neighbor or relative will greatly improve the look of your finished project. For this project, let's assume that you are in a hurry and just want the thing to float and be finished in a weekend.

First, purchase some one-sixth-inch (four-millimeter) thick marine plywood. You will need two pieces that are one foot (30 centimeters) wide and eight feet (two and a half meters) long for the sides. A similarly long but wider piece is also needed for the bottom. Increase the length if you are planning on always traveling with a friend.

Place the side pieces down, one on top of the other. Now, take out your trusty drill and make five holes through both pieces at the short ends, about one inch (two and a half centimeters) from the end. Try to make these holes evenly spaced. Tie some wire or cable ties to hold the wood together temporarily, keeping the loose ends on the inside.

You can now stretch open the side pieces and place them on top of your bottom piece. This should be wide enough to seat you comfortably in the canoe.

Decide how wide your canoe should be. You should of course consider your own girth. If you are a novice, you may wish to make it a little wider, as it will be more stable. If you make it narrower, it will be more likely to capsize but easier to turn.

Draw a line on the bottom piece around your side panels once you are happy with how wide you want them to stretch. You will need to cut the bottom piece to size. Now, drill holes spaced one foot (30 centimeters) apart around the bottom piece of plywood and corresponding holes in the side pieces and use your wire or cable ties to join them together temporarily. Insert a stick or a crossbar between the sides to better stabilize your boat's shape.

You will now need to seal all the seams of your boat—both inside and outside—with a resin that is suitable for boats and fiberglass tape. Allow the resin to dry. You can now cut out your cable ties and sand and varnish your boat.

Once your boat is dry, you can take it out on the water. Don't forget to bring a paddle or two and wear a life jacket.

CANVAS OR FIBERGLASS CANOE

If you do not fancy cutting and measuring, it is possible to buy a canvas canoe kit to make yourself. Fiberglass canoes will require purchasing a fiberglass kit and a mold of a canoe, which can also be built by you. You will end up with a sleek-looking vessel, but it could be quite expensive to build.

BIRCHBARK CANOE

To build a birchbark canoe, you must first find a large birch tree to provide a single piece of bark that is the size of your canoe. Make two horizontal cuts and one vertical cut into the bark and peel it off carefully from the trunk.

You need to make a skeleton for your boat. Cut small pieces of white cedar to act as ribs, and long planks of cedar to line the inside of the canoe. Other pieces can be cut to make seats. Now, find some roots from a nearby cedar tree to use as thread for stitching your bark. You need to fold the bark around your cedar planks, stretch it, and fix it in place. Use the rib pieces to support the planks and the bark. This will take patience and skill. If you succeed, you will have an impressive and very authentic canoe.

An even more time-consuming and time-honored method is to use a whole tree trunk that is burned and dug out with the cunning use of shells. You can, of course, cheat and use metal-edged tools when no one is looking.

First, find a tree and cut or, if you are shunning metal, burn it at the base to fell it. Leave it for three months or so to dry out. You may happen upon an already felled redwood of suitable size; other trees that are suitable include elm, oak, chestnut, or tulip.

Now, apply resin to one side of the tree and set fire to it, being careful to control the burning. Periodically put out the fire and, using your handmade tools, cut away the charred wood. Light the fire again and repeat the process until you have created your canoe. This can be turned into a very open canoe to fit a large number of people or can be more closed in like a kayak. It can have seating or a shaped prow; it can be deep with high sides or very simple. You will have plenty of time to consider these questions of style in the month or more it will take you to dig out your trunk.

70
HOW TO SAIL (TACK AND JIBE)

It is important that you are fully versed in the particulars of sailing your boat before you set out. If you are a novice sailor, you should practice on small inland lakes until you gain competency. Sailing with more experienced people is the best way to learn. Here are some basic tips on sailing.

SETTING OUT

Before setting out, you need to check the rigging. These are the ropes and wires that support your mast.

If you do not have a wind direction indicator, tie some old VHS tape a foot (30 centimeters) below the top of your mast. This will enable you to adjust your sails to the wind effectively.

To set out, point your boat into the wind and hoist the sails.

You cannot sail directly into the wind and must take an angle of about 45 degrees off the wind. To start off well, turn so that the sailboat is 90 degrees off the wind. If you tilt too much, release the tension of the mainsheet a little until your boat is only tilting about 15 degrees.

You need to change direction continually and readjust your sails to match the wind. Trim the sails until they start to flap, then tighten them until they stop. If the sails are left to flap, you will lose power and damage them over time. Do not overtighten the sails.

BEST POSITION

The most efficient or fastest position for your boat is with the wind at your aft quarter, or at your back and side. This is called broad reach.

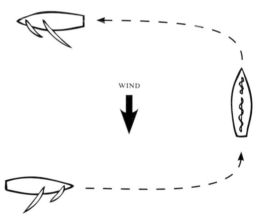

WIND

TACK

You do not always want to go in the direction that the wind is blowing. To turn or change direction when sailing, you need to tack or jibe.

Tacking is turning so that the boat is momentarily face-on to the wind.

If you do this incorrectly, you risk stalling,

known as being "caught in irons." To avoid this, you should pick up speed before turning. If you turn too quickly, the jib (if you are sailing this type of boat) may become snagged. If you are sailing a small vessel and you oversteer, you risk capsizing. You should practice with all of the crew to avoid these problems and to keep up speed while you tack.

Call out "ready about" to alert all crew you are about to turn. On a small boat, you may need to duck under the mast to the other side when turning. "Hard alee" will tell the crew you are turning to the lee side. Once the boat turns out of the wind, you can steer your new course. If you are on a boat with a jib sheet, you will need to release it and then, once you have turned, tie it to the other side quickly so that it fills with wind. Larger boats may have the jib sheet attached to a winch that you will need to crank so that the sail is trimmed and ready for the new heading.

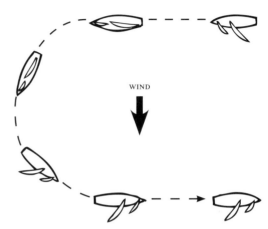

WIND

JIBE

The jibe is another method of turning. It involves using a zigzag pattern of movement. This means you are lengthening your course, but you do not turn into the wind, and there is no risk of stalling. As you retain your speed, the time lost in traveling the extra distance is usually balanced out.

This method is often preferred by sailing racers for this reason.

As the sail is always fully filled with wind, it can result in the boom and mainsail swinging at high speeds across the boat. If the warning "ready to jibe" is not given to the crew, serious injury can occur. Small boats can capsize after attempting to jibe in high winds due to helmsman error and the loss of direction control.

Boats can also be subject to an accidental jibe, which can lead it to capsize or cause injury to crew who are hit by the mainsail swinging wildly. This can be avoided. Never sail your boat directly downwind except for very brief periods. Even small changes in wind or boat direction can cause the wind to flip the mainsail.

71
FISH AT SEA

Deep-sea fishing takes place away from land in waters of at least 100 feet (30 meters) in depth. You may be able to catch fish like sharks, tuna, and swordfish.

TIPS

The sea is a big place. Take note of seabirds hovering above the water. This is usually a good sign of the presence of small fish. Small fish will attract the bigger predatory fish that you want to catch.

If you are fishing for tuna, you will need to be careful, as they are often confused with dolphins. Dolphin fishing is not permitted in most places in the world.

Reefs often attract large fish and are good as deep-sea fishing spots.

If you are not an experienced deep-sea fisherman or an avid sailor, take some motion sickness medication with you. Once the boat comes to a stop, it will rock and bob constantly. You will not have an enjoyable fishing experience if you are ill. If you are prone to seasickness, this may not be the sport for you.

Do not go deep-sea fishing without someone who is experienced. Larger fish can be difficult and dangerous to land.

WHERE TO GO

The best places to go deep-sea fishing in North America include Canada, Cancun, Hawaii, Florida, Alaska, and St. Lucia. In Europe, consider Ireland, England, the Canary Islands, Iceland, and Scandinavia. In Asia, consider heading to the Andaman Islands to catch some barracuda, tuna, or sharks. In Africa, Gambia, South Africa, and Senegal are among the best places to go. In Central America, Costa Rica and El Salvador are good options. Pick a continent and plan your fishing holiday based on what you would prefer to catch.

FISH FOR SHARKS

Remember that you must fish responsibly. Many areas recommend a catch-and-release fishing method when hunting sharks so that the population is not depleted.

Do not attempt to fish for sharks in a small boat. A vessel of at least 35 feet (10 meters) is recommended.

Sharks are attracted by blood, so you need to use bait that floods the water with blood. Some good choices include tuna, eels, or stingrays. The larger the shark, the more bait you will need. For a shark of more than eight feet (two and a half meters) in length, you will need a bait of 15 pounds (seven kilograms) in weight.

Use Styrofoam or plastic balloons to float your bait. You are trying to get the shark to come close to the surface of the water.

You will need strong steel leader wire attached to the end of your fishing line and strong hooks to catch a shark. Sharks will detect the metal. To ensure that they still go for the bait, use plastic-coated wire and wrap your hook with tape.

To catch a shark that is more than eight feet (two and a half meters) long, you will want to cast your hook down to a depth of eight to 15 feet (two and a half to four and a half meters).

Reel in your bait every five minutes to ensure the bait is still on the line.

Brace yourself, and once you feel the shark biting, hold the reel with one hand and the rod with the other. Dip your fishing pole toward the water as you reel in. Lock the reel every 60 seconds to prevent the line from breaking.

If the shark is fighting, allow some give and then reel in again. Repeat this process to tire out the shark. If you have a very large shark on your line, you may need a friend to assist you.

Once you are able to see the shark near the surface, you will need to call for help. A net will be necessary if the shark is small. Use hooks and poles to bring the shark onto the boat if it is too large for a net. Do not use your hands.

When you catch the shark, you must be very cautious. Sharks are strong and have a lot of sharp teeth. Have a heavy bat on hand in case of emergencies.

If you plan to put the shark back in the water, you need to be careful not to injure it when you are releasing it. Wedge open the mouth of the shark with a hammer while you remove the hook.

72
PLANS FOR RESCUE AT SEA

When traveling by boat, you should have a supply of equipment in case of a crisis and to aid rescue. These should include at least three red flares, an inflatable raft, life jackets, lights, whistles, a horn, a radio or satellite equipment, a first aid kit, and a fire extinguisher.

SIGNALING

In order to be rescued, you must be able to signal your position to passing vessels. Do not waste your flares. First, establish that you can actually see a vessel on the horizon. During the day, use red smoke flares, as these will be most visible. At night, use a red flare and leave an interval before using another. You can signal using lights and your horn as well. Stay on your vessel and out of the water for as long as possible and ensure everyone is wearing a life jacket.

DURING THE RESCUE

There are many different scenarios that could occur during a sea rescue. You could be attempting to board a large container or cruise ship from your rig, you could be lifted by a helicopter, or you could be attempting to board a vessel from a dinghy or from the sea. The main factor in your

survival for all of these rescue scenarios is your level of fitness.

Coming alongside a larger vessel in calm seas and attempting to climb aboard is exhausting. Attempting the same feat after many hours of signaling for help and in rough seas requires strength and stamina. You may have a 40-foot (12-meter) sheer climb up a ladder or rope to get you to safety.

Helicopter rescues need different preparation. If you are on your vessel or in a raft, you need to ensure that all equipment is stowed or tied down. If a line is dropped from a helicopter, it is essential that no one touches it until it lands, either on the vessel or on the sea. Static buildup on the line will give you a bad electric shock if you touch it while it dangles.

SINKING

If your boat is sinking quickly or you are thrown overboard, you will not be able to signal calmly for help. Your first priority should be to tie yourself to anything that is more buoyant than you. This is ideally a life jacket or life raft, but may be debris from the vessel. Before you abandon ship, try to grab as many useful supplies as possible. Water, food, any means of signaling, extra clothing and waterproofs, a plastic bag, and a knife are all useful as you bob along on your raft. The food and water have obvious uses. The extra clothes may help keep you warm and dry or prevent sunburn and dehydration. A plastic bag may be rigged to collect rainwater, or to keep extra clothing or food dry. A knife may enable you to kill a seabird that lands on your raft to use as bait for fish. You should attempt to stay alert, calm, and occupied while awaiting rescue. Do not needlessly deplete your supplies. Try to fish, gather water, and make your raft comfortable and assume that you may have to wait for rescue.

SHOCK

There is a real risk of suffering from shock or hypothermia during sea rescue. Someone needs to take charge of all supplies, including food, water, and flares. If anyone in the party starts shivering uncontrollably, behaving oddly, or acting incoherent, action should be taken quickly. Ensure that the person is kept warm, dry, and calm and given a high-sugar snack. If they are conscious, raise the person's legs higher than their head and have them rest. Staying calm and in control will greatly increase your chances of boarding any rescue vessel safely.

73
SURVIVE WHEN A SHARK APPEARS

SHARKS

Most sharks will not attack humans, and if they do so, it only proves fatal about 15 percent of the time. Your chances of drowning are far higher. You are most likely to succumb to a shark attack off the coasts of Australia, Florida, or South Africa. There are four species of sharks to watch for specifically, as they are most often blamed for such attacks—the great white shark, well-known for its appearance in the film *Jaws*; the tiger shark; the bull shark; and the oceanic whitetip. Of course, it is possible to be attacked by other types of sharks and to be killed elsewhere in the world by a shark, so remain vigilant. Other sharks to be extremely wary of include the hammerhead, the blue shark, the blacktip shark, and the mako shark.

AVOID A SHARK ATTACK

Try to avoid swimming in water known to hold sharks. If you must swim, make sure you have others with you or watching you from the shore. Staying within your depth close to shore will not prevent you from being bitten or attacked. Sharks will attack in as little as two feet (60 centimeters) of water.

Do not swim where fish have been discarded into the water or near where shark prey like seals swim.

Do not swim at night or at dusk, as sharks tend to feed and are more aggressive at these times.

HOW TO BEHAVE
WHEN FACED WITH A SHARK

Shark attacks are not all similar. A shark may attack and bite and then leave. You are most likely to survive this attack, as it is due to the shark mistaking you for prey, and then realizing its mistake. You will probably not even see the shark to identify its type. You should try to signal to other swimmers or people on the shoreline for help and try to swim to shallow water immediately.

Sometimes sharks sneak up and attack, biting you repeatedly. These attacks are usually fatal, as you will not have any time to react or call for help.

Luckily, some sharks will choose to approach and bump you, swim away, and then attack. If you are approached and bumped by a shark, you should always assume an attack is imminent.

TAKE ACTION

If you see a shark of any type swimming nearby, leave the area quickly while avoiding sudden panicked movements, as the shark may confuse you with injured prey. If you are unable to leave and the shark swims aggressively toward you or bumps you and swims away, you must prepare for an attack. Attempt to signal for help while staying aware of where the shark is. Stay facing the shark. You need to prevent the shark from biting into your torso. As the shark attacks, you should try to use your arms and legs to keep the shark away, even at the risk of being bitten. Should the shark bite and keep hold of any part of you, do not hit its nose. This works with dogs and alligators, but not sharks. It is much more effective to stick your fingers into the shark's eye sockets and gills. Use as much force as you can and act as quickly as you can. You may not be able to avoid the first bite, but this is survivable. If you fight enough, you may dissuade the shark from returning to bite again.

HOPE

Do not give up hope. Sharks generally bite prey and then move away, returning to eat when they are dead. Even if you are bitten badly, the shark will probably leave you to bleed for a while, giving you time to paddle your way to shore and wave your remaining arm to signal for help. Try not to panic until you leave the water. Excessive splashing while bleeding may attract other predatory sharks.

BOOK SIX

MOUNTAINS

74
HIKE ON HILLS AND MOUNTAINS

Hiking on hills and mountains has both its own charms and its own dangers. The beauty of the scenery and the pleasing challenge of the hike entice many walkers to tackle higher altitudes. You need to ensure that you are properly equipped, have planned your trip, and have a contingency plan for emergencies.

WEATHER

Weather forecasts need to be heeded before setting out on a hike up a mountain, and the more local the forecast the better. It is possible for warm sunshine to give way to freezing fog, heavy rainfall, hailstones, or even snow as you climb. Pack and plan your trip according to the weather, and then assume that it may be a lot worse than predicted; take along supplies that allow for this.

Mist and poor visibility on hills and mountains make getting lost a real danger. Ensure that you are using a map and compass and are regularly taking your bearings. This should allow you to continue with some degree of certainty as to your direction should poor weather obscure landmarks.

Keep an eye on the weather as you hike. Watch for a change in clouds, or any sudden change in either wind force or direction. Sudden changes in wind can be a telling sign that weather is about to change.

PLAN YOUR ROUTE

In order to plan your supplies, you need to sit down with a detailed map of the area you wish to hike and plan your route before you set out. Each time the map indicates steep contour lines, add time to your journey for extra rests. Underestimating the time it will take to reach your destination may leave you short on supplies or without a tent as it gets dark. You will only travel as fast as the least fit person in your group. Each time you climb a hill or mountain, you need to plan an alternate route to descend quickly in case of bad weather or an emergency. Ensure that these routes are clearly marked on your map so that you can use your compass to direct you if you need to descend due to poor visibility. Local knowledge of the terrain will help you plan your route with greater confidence. Try to speak to someone who has hiked in the area in the past for ideas on the preferred route.

TIMING

You should time your hike to start early in the morning. This will allow you to get underway using the most daylight. In winter, you should plan to reach your destination before 4:00 p.m. After this time, you will notice a significant drop in temperature and it will begin to get dark. Hiking at night in any terrain can be hazardous; on hills and mountains it is dangerous and should not

be attempted. It is far safer to stop, create a makeshift shelter, and wait until dawn to continue with your hike.

GETTING LOST

It is very possible to get lost despite the best planning and the use of maps and a compass. The moment you realize that you are not on your expected trail, stop walking and observe your surroundings. Think carefully back to the last time you were sure you were not lost. Check your map and look for features that you should be able to see if you are nearby—high ground and valleys, for instance. Do not look around and try to match the map to what you see, as this may lead you off track. Finding a river on the map and then convincing yourself that it is the one beside you, without referencing the surrounding landscape for other landmarks from the map, will lead you to falsely identify your position. Once you have recognized features from the map, use your compass to get your bearings and return to your hike. Do not continue to walk until you are absolutely sure you know where you are and in which direction you should be walking.

Try to remain calm. If you have left your estimated time of arrival and your route card with a ranger or a reliable friend and packed your supplies well, you know you can survive and will be rescued.

CLOTHING AND SUPPLIES

When hiking on high ground, even if you are going on a one-day hike, you need to pack extra supplies. In addition to your compass, map, fire-lighting supplies, knife, and torch, you will need extra clothing, emergency food, daily rations, a first aid kit, a 98-foot (30-meter) rope about half an inch (13 millimeters) thick, and a survival bag. Always pack waterproofs and a wool hat. This will enable you to stay dry and warm if it gets dark and you are lost and awaiting rescue.

When packing food, you need to be aware of weight and nutritional needs. Running out of food halfway to your destination is not ideal. You should expect to eat up to two and a half pounds (one kilogram) of food in a day hiking 10 to 30 miles (15 to 45 kilometers). If you plan to hike over a number of days and travel a distance of 100 miles (160 kilometers), you may need to consider resupplying your food en route.

75
PREPARE FOR ALTITUDE AND MOUNTAINEERING

As you grow more adventurous in your hiking, you may consider higher trails or even mountaineering. You need to be prepared for the challenges of hiking at altitude.

HOW HIGH

A high-altitude hike takes you between 8,000 and 13,000 feet (2,500 and 4,000 meters). A very high-altitude hike would be from 13,000 to 18,000 feet (4,000 to 5,500 meters). In most places, this would entail climbing skills and there would not be trails. Anything higher than 18,000 feet (5,500 meters) is mountaineering and requires specialist breathing equipment due to the low levels of oxygen. For every 1,000 feet (300 meters) you climb, there is three percent less oxygen in the air.

AIR TEMPERATURE

In addition to loss of oxygen, you will also experience lower air temperatures as you ascend. On average, the temperature will drop three and a half degrees Fahrenheit (two degrees Celsius) for every 1,000 feet (300 meters) you climb. When preparing for your hike, study your map carefully and calculate what temperature you will experience at the height of your hike. This estimate does not take into account wind, rain, or snow, which will make you feel even colder.

HOW TO HIKE AT ALTITUDE

To ensure that you are taking in enough oxygen from the air, you will need to breathe deeper and more often to prevent exhaustion and to enable you to continue. You will need to hike at a slower pace and to establish a rhythm of steps and breaths. If you find yourself becoming breathless, immediately slow your pace and take deeper breaths. If you are walking up a steep slope, take a deep breath for each step you take. This should ensure that you maintain your hike and reach your goal. Extra warm clothes, sunglasses, and sunscreen are also essential to ensure you remain comfortable. Expect to take extra breaks for rest and factor these rests into your time estimates for reaching your destination.

ALTITUDE SICKNESS

While walking and breathing correctly may prevent exhaustion, they will not prevent altitude sickness.

Altitude sickness occurs when your body reacts to a sudden change in altitude.

Ascending too fast will cause altitude sickness. If you are habitually living in a low-lying place and decide to go on a high-altitude hike, you need to acclimate your body before you set out. Spending a night at a higher altitude before starting your hike may prepare your body enough to avoid symptoms. Some people are more prone to altitude sickness, but anyone can suffer from it, regardless of how well they have managed high-altitude climbs in the past.

You should be aware of the symptoms and take time to acclimate to any hike higher than 8,000 feet (2,500 meters).

Signs of altitude sickness include nausea, lack of interest in food or drink, headache, dizziness, a lack of coordination, and shortness of breath. You will not be able to continue on your hike if your symptoms persist.

To reduce the symptoms of altitude sickness, you need to descend, drink a lot of water even though you may not feel thirsty, and slow your pace down or consider resting for one hour.

Most people suffer mild symptoms once they go higher than 10,000 feet (3,000 meters). If symptoms get worse, however, action must be taken immediately. Altitude sickness can be fatal. Early signs include nausea and a headache. This will be followed by exhaustion. All of these symptoms may occur normally simply as a result of exertion at high altitude. If resting, drinking, eating, and taking an analgesic does not relieve your headache or tiredness, you should assume that you are suffering from altitude sickness.

At this point, you should plan an immediate descent of at least 1,500 feet (500 meters) and rest again. If you are still unwell or other symptoms occur, call for help and, if you are able to hike, continue your descent.

More serious symptoms include disorientation and a loss of coordination. High altitude can result in fluid in the lungs. The signs of this will include shortness of breath or coughing up fluid. You need to call for help immediately. Fluid may also gather on the brain, resulting in disorientation, and will progressively get worse over a number of days. This is very serious and you will need to call for rescue and descend quickly to prevent death.

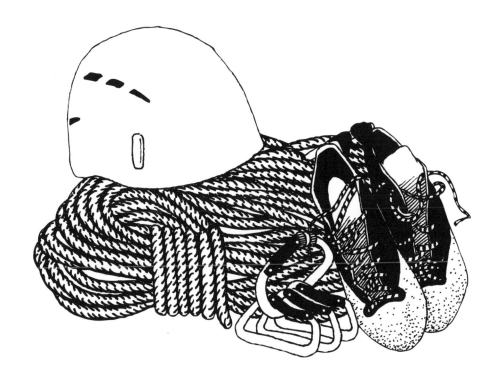

76
PLAN ROUTES AND CLIMB WITH ROPES

When setting out on your expedition on hilly or mountainous terrain, you should bring ropes and basic climbing equipment. You may plan a route on a trail with no climbing but then find yourself stuck, lost, or in need of changing your course due to incoming bad weather. Then you will need ropes.

Basic climbing equipment should include the following:

- 200 to 230 feet (60 to 70 meters) of dynamic climbing rope
- A harness
- Climbing shoes
- Three or more carabiners
- 15 extenders or quick draws
- Passive protection or a climbing rack (the equipment to enable you to anchor to the rock during your climb)

Do not attempt to climb using anything other than proper climbing ropes. Short climbs on rocks with easy handholds may be attempted in dry conditions without ropes. This is known as scrambling. Higher, steeper climbs or any climb in wet weather should involve the use of ropes for safety.

First, you need to plan your climbing route by carefully surveying the rock and visualizing each move you will make. It is unlikely that you will have a rope already anchored and lowered for your benefit when you are exploring. The fittest and most experienced climber should ascend and bring a rope to anchor to the top. As with rappeling, great care should be taken in finding a secure anchor and tying a knot well. It is best to create two anchors. If you have the equipment and the size of the climb warrants it, intermediate anchors should be set into the rock face on the way up.

A spotter should stay below to help catch the first climber or at least protect their head and neck should they fall. Subsequent climbers will have the safety of the rope. Never attempt to catch a falling climber who has gone higher than your head height, and never try to catch them by pushing them toward the rock face, as this could lead to additional injuries.

CLIMBING TECHNIQUE

There are five parts of the body engaged when climbing: your torso, your two hands, and your two feet. Three points of contact should be kept with the rock face at all times. Do not overstretch your arms, but keep them level with your shoulders. Use foot movements more regularly than hand movements. Once you have moved your feet a few times, you will be able to stretch up and then move your hands up. This will ensure that you are using your legs to hold your weight and not your arms or hands. If you try to pull up with your arms, you risk getting fatigued and getting cramps in your hands.

Keep your body close to the rock, but far enough away to allow you to see where you are going. Keep in a slightly crouched position and do not overstretch. Do not rest on your elbows or knees. Keep your feet as flat against the rock as possible.

If there are three or more people planning to climb and it is a high climb, consider climbing in stages. Once the first climber has reached a certain height, they set an anchor and wait for the rest of the climbing party to reach them. A different climber can take the lead for the next stretch. This will make the process faster and eliminate fatigue and stress for the first climber. This is known as multi-pitching.

SAFETY

Apart from when you are using a spotter, you should not climb with anyone directly below or above you.

If you encounter loose rocks, do not disturb them with your hands or rope. Loose rocks can cause serious injury to those below, even when they are small. If rocks are dislodged, shout a warning to anyone below. Wearing helmets will protect climbers from injuries of this type. You should never look straight up when climbing; always look straight ahead.

Do not attempt a climb in wet or windy weather unless you are fully equipped and experienced, and there is no other way to reach your destination.

Before climbing, remove all rings, watches, and gloves. Unless you are climbing in extremely cold weather, gloves will impede your process. Rings may cause problems if your fingers swell, and watches may snag on a rock and cause you to slip.

Make sure that your clothing is not likely to snag on loose rocks.

Check your boots and remove any mud from the grooves in the sole. If the soles are wet, dry them before setting out.

If you fall, try to stay close to the rock and slow your fall by getting a foothold. Try not to panic; shout a falling warning to those below. If the rope is properly anchored, it will save you from a continuous fall.

When climbing, you should avoid loose vegetation and moss.

Plan your climb with the weakest member of your party in mind.

77

RAPPEL

To rappel is to descend down a rock face in a controlled manner using ropes. It is used by mountain climbers and also is a hobby in its own right.

WHAT TO WEAR

In order to rappel, you will need to wear protective clothing. A helmet is essential. Elbow and kneepads will protect you from any hard knocks during your descent. Gloves are often worn by beginners, although these are not favored by experienced climbers. A climbing harness and good shoes or boots with grips will help protect your feet and prevent you from slipping and banging into the cliff face. You should ideally use a static rope for rappeling.

SAFETY

Rappeling is a dangerous activity, especially if you are undertaking it under emergency conditions. You need to proceed with caution and double-check your knots and anchors. Nearly a quarter of all climbing accidents occur during rappeling. Most of these are caused by rappeling beyond the length of the rope or by the anchor slipping. If you are climbing or rappeling in an established place, a permanent anchor may be provided. Otherwise, take time to secure your anchor. Unless you are using a 200-year-old oak tree, create two anchors and test them first by using your full body weight.

GETTING READY TO GO WITH ONLY A ROPE

Find a place to tie your anchor. Always tie two anchors. A tree or large boulders are ideal. Avoid tying your rope to anything that has sharp, jagged edges. If you are body rappeling in an emergency, a second rope will reduce the friction burn on your hands and body as you descend. Knot the rope to the anchor with care. If your ropes are of equal width, use a simple overhand or reef knot, also known as a square knot. If your ropes are different sizes, use a double fisherman's knot in conjunction with a reef knot. It is essential that your knot does not slip. If you have only one rope and it is long enough, double it over and simply loop it around a tree or boulder. This will enable you to retrieve your rope when you get to the bottom.

Now you need to fix the ropes. Face the anchor and pass the rope between your legs. Then, bring the rope around your body on the left and pass over your right shoulder so that it drops behind you. Use your right hand behind you to hold the rope and your left hand in front of you. Drop the rope down the cliff face and check to make sure it has not snagged.

TAKE OFF

The greatest strain on the anchor will occur during the first few steps of your rappel, so go slowly. Stand with your feet planted apart and lean backward. You need to lean back quite far to prevent slipping, which would result in your face slamming into the cliff face. Walk backward until you are well over the edge. Do not attempt to hold your body weight with your left hand; allow the ropes to take your weight and manage your descent by slowly allowing the ropes to pass through your hands.

FRICTION

If you are rappeling as a hobby, you will be fully equipped with proper safety equipment. If you are descending in an emergency, you will probably not have any equipment. You may need to protect your hands with gloves, and ensure that your groin and shoulders are well padded with clothes. There is no safety net in rappeling, especially in an emergency. Place something under the ropes at the cliff top to prevent them from snagging and breaking from friction as you descend.

LANDING

If you are unsure whether or not your rope is long enough, it is best not to begin a descent. To ensure that you cannot fall off the end of the rope, or miscalculate where you are, tie a large knot at the end.

78
HANG GLIDE

A hang glider is a modified parachute, a flexible wing in a triangular shape, with cables and tubes that make it rigid. The air flowing over the surface causes it to rise, lifting you in the air with it. When you travel using a hang glider, you are really falling in a slow, hopefully very controlled way.

PREPARATION

Before attempting to hang glide, you should always seek professional guidance and have all of your equipment checked thoroughly. In addition to your hang glider, you need to be dressed in clothes to protect you from the cold air and the elements. Eye protection, gloves, and a helmet are necessary. If you are planning to travel at high altitude, a reserve parachute is recommended, as well as an insulated flight bag.

Shifts in the position of the pilot of the hang glider affect the direction and speed of it. The pilot is suspended from the center of the glider in a harness or flight bag and holds a pole, or control bar, that lies beneath their shoulders. If you are the pilot and you wish to turn the glider left, simply shift your weight to the left; to turn right, lean your body to the right.

In order to speed up the hang glider, pull the control bar beneath you toward you, tipping the nose of the glider down. To slow down, simply push the pole forward, which pulls up the nose of the glider. If you speed up too much or tip the nose of the glider forward too far, you may descend too fast and crash. If you pull the nose of the glider up too far, the glider may stall. When you stall, all gliding stops and is replaced by dropping at speed, accompanied by some appropriate screaming and panic. It is best not to stall unless you are very close to the ground.

To start out, you will need to assemble the hang glider and have someone strap you correctly into it. It is best to start at the top of a slight incline. Ensure that the path ahead is clear of large rocks, people, or other obstacles. Grab hold of the side poles of the control bar, lift the hang glider, and start to run. Once you reach a speed of 15 mph (25 kph) or more, the glider will begin to lift off the ground. Then move your hands to the center of the control bar.

It is best at first either to try hang gliding in tandem with an instructor or to take a class. Your first flight will probably be quite short and at low altitude to allow you to master keeping your hang glider level, controlling your speed, and landing on your

feet. In order to land, you must stall the hang glider by pushing the control bar away from you. At the same time, as the ground approaches, you must drop your feet. Your aim is to slow the hang glider gradually as you approach the ground so that you only need to take a few quick steps when your feet hit the ground before you stop. The hang glider will weigh more than 60 pounds (25 kilograms). You should not expect to land feetfirst on your first try.

MORE ADVANCED FLYING TECHNIQUES

The force of gravity is constantly at work, in conjunction with the weight of the glider, to slow you down and bring you back to earth. To turn what is otherwise a very short flight into a true adventure, you will need to use updrafts and thermals to keep you aloft.

If you locate hot air rising off the ground (thermals) and fly your hang glider over them, they will lift you in the air. The sun creates thermals by shining on sand, rock, or concrete, which absorb its heat. Columns of hot air rise

from these surfaces. Birds use thermals to stay aloft and conserve their energy. You can find thermals by observing birds.

Updrafts are also a useful way of gaining altitude and lengthening your flight. Updrafts occur when wind hits a ridge or hill and is pushed upward.

In addition to using these techniques, more advanced hang gliders will usually take off from higher ground or from mountains.

BEWARE

Always wear safety gear and check all of your equipment before setting out. Pack an emergency parachute for high-altitude flights. Carry an altimeter to keep track of your altitude and a variometer to show your climb or descent rate.

Avoid overcorrecting when you are attempting to speed up, slow down, or even change direction. Instead make continual small adjustments.

Avoid all obstacles, power lines, trees, and mountains. It is best to avoid all thermals and updrafts until you have mastered the basic techniques thoroughly.

Turbulent air can cause the hang glider to tumble. It is very difficult to regain control and level the glider when this happens.

Carry a small first aid kit with you, a knife in case you crash and become entangled in your glider, and a radio or cell phone should you need assistance upon landing.

79
FORAGE FOR PROVISIONS AT ALTITUDE

If you find yourself on a snowy mountain peak, you will not be able to forage for food. First, you will need to descend to a valley where some trees or greenery are present. As with all foraging, being open-minded will ensure a balanced meal.

EAT THE TREES

At high altitudes, animal and plant life is naturally scarcer. You may have to consider eating pine needles or beech bark. This will not provide a tasty or particularly nutritious meal, but may stave off starvation and severe hunger pangs while you look for other food.

MUSHROOMS

Some mushrooms can be toxic and no form of preparation will make them safe to eat. That insects are feeding on a mushroom is no indication that it is safe for humans to eat. Unless you are an experienced mushroom picker, do not eat them.

BERRIES

Berries from bushes and trees may be eaten once you clearly identify them. Food that is safe for birds may cause illness in humans. If you are unsure of the berry, it is best to avoid it. Berries that are OK to eat include black raspberries, red mulberries, blackberries, fox grapes, and huckleberries. Red berries from the rowan tree are high in vitamin C and safe to eat.

Huckleberries

NUTS

You may also find nuts that are edible if you find yourself in a mixed hardwood forest. These include black walnuts, white or butternut walnuts, and hazelnuts. Do not eat any nuts that you cannot safely identify or any that look bad, contain mold, or have broken shells. Acorns can be gathered, shelled, and ground to make coarse flour that can be added to your cooking to bulk it up.

MEAT

If you perceive tracks or notice birds or small mammals, consider setting up traps or hunting. Birds may also be used to find fresh water or, in the spring and early summer, you may retrieve eggs from their nests and eat them. Predatory animals like wolves, foxes, and bears are difficult to find and hard to catch and kill. You risk injury to yourself. You would be better setting traps to catch smaller mammals, like mice or squirrels.

INSECTS

Insects may be abundant regardless of the season at higher altitudes and may provide a high-protein snack on your hike. Turn over logs on the ground and look under rotting vegetation. Millipedes are easy to find and good to eat. Centipedes, which have only two legs, not four, on each segment of their bodies, will bite and are best avoided. Worms should be soaked in cold water to purge them and then cooked before eating.

FISH

It is difficult but possible to catch fish by hand. Sit on a rock in shallow water and make sure your shadow does not fall on the water. Wait for a fish. Grab the fish by pushing it down into the riverbed. You can also sharpen a stick and make a fishing spear. If you have a net, stretch it across a shallow river until you trap fish and then retrieve them.

Try not to get wet while fishing, and remove and replace all wet clothing immediately to prevent hypothermia.

A stream or river well supplied with fish may attract bears, so watch for any tracks and proceed with caution.

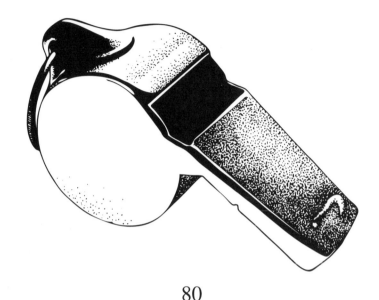

80
GET RESCUED FROM HILLS AND MOUNTAINS

Hiking in the hills and mountains, or at high altitude, should not be undertaken without preparation and planning for potential rescue. A simple ankle sprain that would cause only a minor inconvenience on a summer hike at low altitude could prove fatal in bad weather at high altitude.

SAFETY IN NUMBERS
Traveling in a group of at least four is the best preparation. There should never be fewer than three people in your group. If anyone falls ill from hypothermia, is injured from a fall, or suffers from altitude sickness, you will then have the option of sending

someone for help. One person should stay with the injured party. If an ankle injury has occurred, do not remove the hiking boot, as it will work as a splint. If someone is suffering from shock, hypothermia, or another sickness, treat it appropriately. A tent or makeshift shelter should be erected, and the victim should be kept calm, warm, and fed. Use your survival bag and your waterproofs. If a fracture is suspected, or any injury that may require surgery, and you know that help will arrive soon, do not feed the patient.

Refer to a compass and map to get clear details of your position. This information, as well as a written account of the injury or illness, should be carried by anyone setting out to get help so that mountain rescue personnel can act swiftly.

LEAVE A CLEAR ITINERARY

Clearly mapping and leaving behind a statement of your proposed route, your estimated time of arrival at your destination, and any alternate routes is important. Make up a route card. These details should be left with someone reliable so that if you are unable to signal for rescue or descend the mountain, you will have someone to alert mountain rescue.

SIGNALING FOR RESCUE

Use as many means to signal for help as possible to increase your chances of being seen. Always signal from a visible place clear of trees or other obstructions, if possible.

Consider packing some rescue essentials, especially if you are planning to hike alone. Many quite isolated areas for hiking have quite good coverage for cell phones so consider bringing yours. If you are going to an isolated area alone, consider renting a satellite phone in case of an emergency. You may also wish to consider investing in a personal locator beacon, which will allow rescuers to find you.

Another item to use is the simple whistle. Blow the whistle in bursts of three, wait one minute to prevent hyperventilating, and repeat.

If it is dark, light three fires in a visible spot. During the day, light a single fire and then place moss or damp greenery on it to create dense smoke that is highly visible. Smoke or signal flares can also be used if you have them.

A mirror or reflective surface can be used to signal distant search planes or helicopters during the day. If you have more than one mirror, hang them from trees or rocks to reflect sunlight so that you are drawing attention to your position even while you are resting.

Find a spot on high ground and use any available materials to write SOS in large letters that will be visible from the air.

WAITING FOR RESCUE

It is important to remain calm and rested while you wait for rescue. You should remain positive about being rescued in a timely manner, while at the same time planning for a lengthy wait. Make preparations for an overnight stay. Build a shelter or erect your tent or use whatever you have to keep out of the wind and rain and stay warm. Build a fire if possible. If you cannot find water, ration what you have. Use your emergency food supplies. Even if you have sent for help or used your cell phone, use signal fires, mirrors, or markers to draw attention to your position.

BOOK SEVEN

SNOW AND ICE

81

PREPARE FOR SNOWY AND ICY TERRAIN

In order to hike, camp, or explore in snow or ice terrain, you will need to have specialized cold weather gear. Sleeping bags and tents should be bought with extreme weather in mind. All clothes, equipment, first aid, and supplies will need to be fit for the task. In addition, you will need to be properly prepared both physically and mentally, and equipped with the knowledge to undertake your expedition.

EQUIPMENT

You will need a hat, insulated gloves, and waterproof outer gloves. Layers of clothing will both insulate you and keep you dry. Appropriate footwear and glasses are also necessary. Extra clothing is essential. Wet clothes must be changed quickly to prevent your core body temperature from dropping. If you plan to travel on ice or slopes, crampons on your hiking shoes and a snow axe are essential. A snow pole will help with walking in snow.

Food and extra emergency rations, a working stove, an extra stove as a backup, and fuel for your stove should all be brought even on short trips.

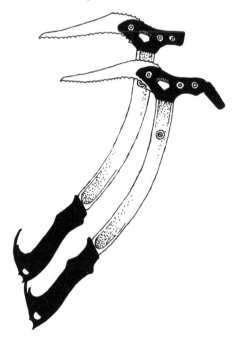

Fig. 1—Crampons

Fig. 2—Ice axes

FIRST AID

Have an appropriate first aid kit with you. A smaller emergency first aid kit should also be carried on your person. If you are traveling on snow and ice for a number of days in isolated areas, each member of your party needs to be able to identify the early symptoms of cold weather illnesses and know some general first aid.

MENTAL ATTITUDE

Traveling in snow and ice leaves you susceptible to accidents, avalanches, being trapped by bad weather, loss of equipment due to mishaps, and various specific illnesses, as well as fatigue. Everyone reacts differently to situations that cause stress, which may be physical or mental. It is a good idea to engage in some short, manageable expeditions in cold weather conditions to increase your self-confidence. It is also advisable to travel with others who are experienced and to ensure that you are well prepared.

It is essential for your safety and survival that you remain calm and in control should the unexpected occur.

PHYSICAL PREPARATION

Hiking or exploring in cold or high-altitude areas requires a high level of fitness. Have a health check-up a couple of months before you plan your trip to allow time to get in shape. You should be fit and not be underweight or overweight. Extreme cold and high altitude puts strain on your circulation, lungs, and heart. Have your cholesterol checked. Quit alcohol, tobacco, and fatty foods and eat healthy foods.

The day before beginning your trip, drink at least 96 ounces (about three liters) of water, and aim to drink a high volume of fluids throughout your trip. Adequate fluid intake, coupled with correct clothing and good fitness, will greatly reduce your chances of suffering from frostbite, hypothermia, and altitude sickness.

82
EXPLORE IN THE SNOW

Walking in snow can be a slow and tiring process. If you truly wish to explore in the snow, you should consider some alternative forms of transport. Cross-country skiing, dog sledding, and snowmobiles are all enjoyable ways to get around in the snow.

CROSS-COUNTRY SKIING
Cross-country skiing is a popular sport and a mode of transport that dates back to the Vikings, and it can be enjoyed by all ages and fitness levels. You will need skis, ski boots, warm waterproof clothing, a hat, sunglasses for snow, and gloves. If you have engaged in downhill skiing before, you should note that there are differences. When you ski downhill, your skis are firmly planted on the ground. In cross-country skiing, the skis are free to move. You move and turn by stepping and gliding.

Lean forward, reach forward with your hand and ski pole, and take a step with each foot alternately. Pause between each step to glide when on a flat or downhill area. Gliding will save energy and enable you to explore further.

When traveling uphill, change to a hopping style. Pause between hops to enable a gliding step. If the incline is too steep, turn your skis outward and take lifting steps. Imagine you are a duck walking uphill, and you will get the correct idea.

To travel downhill, simply change to a skiing technique.

Change direction by using your steps to turn you gradually when on a flat or uphill surface. When you are going downhill, you will need a different method. Lean forward and place your weight on your front foot as you change the direction of the ski. You will be using a method that is more common in roller skating or ice skating. If you do not lean forward, you will end up falling backward. A more advanced method is to lean on the front foot and drop your back knee down, while bringing that ski in line with the turning ski. This will not interrupt your sliding motion and, when mastered, will take less energy.

DOG SLEDDING

If you wish to go faster and are a dog lover, you could consider dog sledding. You will need a dog. All huskies like to pull sleds, but other breeds, such as pointers and hunting dogs, can also be easily trained. You will need the correct type of harness and lines to secure the dog to the sled. If you are using a dog that has no experience with sledding, allow it to get used to wearing the harness and allow it to pull around some light weights until it is familiar with the concept. The dog should be happy to drag around at least a 25-pound (10-kilogram) weight before you tie the animal to a sled. You will also need to teach the dog basic commands.

The command "Gee" (pronounced like the letter G) means turn right and "Haw" means turn left. "Whoa" means stop. "On-by" means the dog should continue past an interesting distraction and then get a treat. "Line out" tells the dog to walk forward until the gang line is taut behind it. Ensure that your dog knows these commands very well before setting out. Then, attach your dog to the sled. It may be necessary to have your children or an elderly neighbor run in front and get the dog to chase them at first.

Remember to keep the line taut. Get ready to put on the brake in case the dog stops obeying your commands or suddenly stops. Wear thick clothing and be prepared to fall off. Remember that a dog is for life and not just for a winter of dog sledding.

SNOWMOBILING

If you are interested in speed or long-range exploring, then a snowmobile is for you. In

Scandinavia, you may drive a snowmobile once you are eligible to drive a car and have a valid driver's license. Check the regulations regarding the use of snowmobiles in the area you are traveling. In some places, you can operate a snowmobile from the age of 12. There may be designated roads or tracks, and speed limits may apply. If you are planning on exploring in Scandinavia, the United States, Canada, or Russia, you should find out about the local clubs and volunteers in the area, as they may have established trails that you can use safely.

You should be aware of both your own abilities and the capabilities of your vehicle and not overreach either. Do not drink alcohol. When you are crossing main roads, always travel at right angles to the traffic. You must wear a helmet at all times, as well as proper clothing and gloves. You should not travel in areas prohibited to snowmobiles and you should respect private property.

Regardless of which method of exploration you choose to use, always let others know your route, destination, and estimated time of arrival. Find out about the area and bring a map and compass with you. Bring emergency supplies, such as food and first aid, and the means to make a fire and signal for help should you become injured or lost.

83
WALK IN THE SNOW

When walking in deep snow, you will need good waterproof hiking boots, waterproof pants, and a hiking pole with a basket attached or a stick you can use to test your way and stabilize yourself as you walk. A snow axe and crampons should be in your backpack and will come in handy should you come across any ice or steep slopes.

Walking on snow can be a slow and laborious task. Walk in the footsteps of the lead walker and change places periodically to reduce fatigue.

If you find yourself walking uphill, use your hiking pole to test the way and kick into the snow. Soft, deep snow may be covering hard, compacted ice, so be prepared. If you are uncertain or the slope is steep, then ascend gradually in a zigzag pattern and be prepared for slips.

WALKING DOWNHILL

If you are walking downhill, you have a few options and can have some fun experimenting with your technique.

You may wish to try the sitting glissade, which involves sitting down and letting yourself slide down the slope. Take out your ice axe to use as a brake and a rudder and test it carefully to make sure the slope is not too steep. If your pants are nylon, this is not advisable, as you may go too fast to be able to stop. Shorts are also not a good idea, as you will end up with friction burns. Do not wear crampons on your boots, as they may catch in the ground and flip you forward onto your face, which may lead to an injury or unsightly friction burns.

If you prefer a more sedate pace when traveling downhill, then the plunge step is the one for you. Lift your leg and keep it straight. Lean back and plunge your straightened leg into the snow heelfirst. Slide forward and then prepare to take the next step. Do not be tempted to go too fast using this method, as you could end up stuck in unexpectedly deep snow or breaking your leg. A steady pace should prevent your forward leg from sinking too deeply into the snow.

Boot skiing is another method of downhill descent in the snow. This involves skiing on your feet, interspersed with taking short steps, and sliding on your feet. The trick is not to lock your knees. Ski poles or two snow poles will help you balance. If you fall back, you can simply change to the sitting glissade method. This method is fun and a quick way to move in the snow, but it requires strong legs.

BEWARE

Do not walk close to trees, as they may hide tree wells. These are deep holes around the base of the tree that have been sheltered from snowfall by lower branches.

Be very careful if you are walking near a ridge or cliff, as snow may obscure or overhang the edge and give way as you walk on it.

Soft snow may cover and insulate streams or rivers and prevent thick ice from forming. Stepping on this snow could result in getting wet or being swept under the ice.

Gullies, ravines, uneven ground, and snow-covered natural or man-made obstacles can cause an injury. Test the way if you are unsure what is ahead and use your snow pole for stability.

If you are walking in an area prone to avalanches, stay alert. Earlier avalanches may result in extremely large drifts of snow or snow-covered debris.

84

JUDGE ICY TERRAIN FOR WALKING AND SKATING

There is a saying that ice testers are found in the spring. If at all possible, make use of local knowledge before venturing out on ice. Being properly equipped with the correct safety gear may literally save your life.

Before going out on ice, ensure that you are properly equipped. Wear cleats or crampons on your shoes. Have a snow axe or make an ice grabber. The trick is to ensure that your descent down an icy slope or into an ice-covered lake can be stopped quickly. Traveling in a group or with one other person will greatly increase your chances of surviving a mishap on the ice. Also consider wearing a float coat and have a metal stick to test the thickness of the ice ahead. A float coat will provide the flotation of a life jacket while allowing mobility and insulating you from the cold.

MAKE AN ICE GRABBER

Take an old broom handle and cut two 10-inch (25-centimeter) pieces. Drill a hole in one end of each piece and insert a spike, allowing it to protrude a couple of inches (about five centimeters). Now, drill a hole close to the other end of each piece and tie a piece of cord or rope long enough so that you can pass it up one sleeve, over your back, and down the other. Your grabbers will dangle at your wrists, ready for gripping the slippery ice at a moment's notice.

In order to create ice safe for travel and skating, you need persistent cold temperatures. A lake must be frozen to a thickness of three or four inches (eight to 10 centimeters) to be safe to walk or skate on. If you are testing new ice with a friend, spread out. If the ice starts to crack under your weight, it will probably still support your weight long enough for you to move to safety.

SAFE ICE

At the start of the winter a lake will start to freeze at the edges, so you'll find the safest ice there. Smaller ponds and lakes, shallow areas of lakes, and sheltered bodies of water will freeze earlier in the season.

When considering whether ice is safe, remember that the colder the weather, the harder the ice will be. Ice will be safer on smaller lakes and ponds. Newer ice is safer than older ice. On larger bodies of water, the ice in the center will remain frozen and safer late in the season, and the ice at the edges will melt first.

ICE TO AVOID

River ice is always more dangerous, as moving water can soften or melt the ice overnight. Bends in the river or underwater currents can greatly affect the safety of the surface ice. Underwater currents running into lakes can also cause the ice to form thinly.

Larger lakes can also be problematic, as they tend to freeze in stages. Ridges in the ice will indicate where new ice has formed. Proceed with caution, as the newer ice beyond the ridge may be too thin to walk or skate on.

Ridges in the ice indicate a weak spot and may be a sign of underwater currents. Do not venture out on ice formed on large bodies of water unless you are in a group and have a flotation device.

Avoid any ice that has snow lying on it. Snow will insulate the ice from the cold. Also watch for greenery or emerging vegetation late in the season, as this will absorb heat, causing the ground to warm and the surrounding ice to melt. Other features, such as rocks, piers, or docks, will also accelerate ice thinning.

Once ice has become old, blackened, or no longer has a flat, sheetlike appearance, avoid it.

85
TRAVEL ON ICY TERRAIN

When walking on ice, you are in a constant battle with gravity. Here are some good techniques to prevent you from sliding down the mountain, or simply landing hard on your face or other, more padded, areas of your body.

WALKING

Always equip yourself with an ice axe and wear crampons, which are grips that attach to your shoes. A walking stick with a sharp end will help keep you stable and enable you to judge the ice ahead. Ensure that your backpack is packed in such a way that you are balanced. Lean slightly forward while you walk. Watch out for slopes or ridges ahead.

UPHILL

It is best to avoid scaling icy inclines and find alternate routes. If there is no other way around, take time to consider whether you should be anchoring yourself to the ice with ropes as you ascend. If you are traveling in a group, you may wish to tie together with a rope to enable others to help you stop if you slip. Do not use this method unless everyone is properly trained in the self-arrest technique explained below.

If there is a steep icy slope ahead, do not take the shortest route to the top. Walk in a zigzag, using your axe to anchor you to the ice as you use kicking steps. Proceed slowly. Do not overstretch with your steps or with your axe.

If you are attempting to walk up a gentler slope, use your walking stick to stabilize yourself.

DOWNHILL

Before attempting a downhill walk on icy terrain, make sure you can see what is at the bottom of the hill. For example, if you slip, are you going to continue off the edge of a mountain? If the slope does not end in a sizable ledge or flat area free of large obstructions, try to find another way to get to your destination. If there are no other options, use ropes to anchor yourself as you descend.

Are you confident that slipping down the icy slope will not be your last act on earth? You should assume that you are likely to slip and prepare yourself. Make sure that there are no loose items hanging off of your clothes or backpack that will entangle you if you fall and slide. Prepare to use the self-arrest technique described below.

If the slope is relatively gentle, walk

forward, digging in your heels and using your stick to keep yourself balanced. Do not walk directly behind anyone.

If the slope is steep and the ice is snow-covered, consider walking backward while pressing the walking stick into the ground in front of you. On compacted ice, use your axe.

SLIPPING AND
SELF-ARREST TECHNIQUE

If you slip, you can use a self-arrest technique. It is best to go to a specialized class to perfect this technique, as there is a danger of impaling yourself on your axe. You can get a friend to show you and practice on a hard-packed snowy slope. Once you are comfortable with using your axe, try again while wearing waterproofs, which will speed your descent. Do not try this for the first time on compacted ice.

- While you walk, hold your axe in the hand closest to the icy slope, with the sharp end pointing forward and away from you.
- If you feel yourself succumbing to gravity, hold the axe against your chest and turn toward the slope.
- Dig the axe into the slope. You will be lying on top of the axe.
- Keep your torso pressed on the axe and on the ice. Try to lift your face off of the ice.

86
BUILD A SLED

A sled is a fun and practical item to have for snowy and icy terrain. There are many designs, shapes, sizes, and prices to consider when purchasing a sled. It is also quite easy to make your own sled if you have a few materials and are enthusiastic.

IF YOU HAVE A TOOLBOX

To make a wooden sled, you will need two six-foot (two-meter) pieces of two-by-four-inch (five-by-10-centimeter) lumber and a sheet of quarter-inch (six-millimeter) plywood 32 inches (80 centimeters) wide and 36 inches (90 centimeters) long. You will also need a table saw, a sander, four wood screws half an inch (125 millimeters) long and four wood screws three inches (seven and a half centimeters) long, and a length of rope.

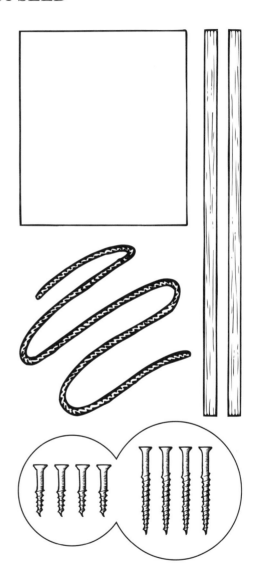

- Cut each of your six-foot (two-meter) pieces of wood into pieces two feet (60 centimeters) and four feet (120 centimeters) long, and make a 45-degree angle cut at the end of each four-foot (120-centimeter) piece. The table saw will do this easily.
- Attach the two four-foot (120-centimeter) runners together using the two-foot (60-centimeter) pieces with the three-inch (seven-and-a-half-centimeter) wood

screws. Attach them approximately two inches (five centimeters) from the end of your runners.

- Place the plywood sheet on top of the runners and attach it to the runners about one foot (30 centimeters) from the front with the half-inch (125-millimeter) wood screws. This forms the seat.
- Drill two holes, one foot (30 centimeters) apart, at the front of the seat sled to attach your rope handle, using knots at the ends of the rope to secure it.

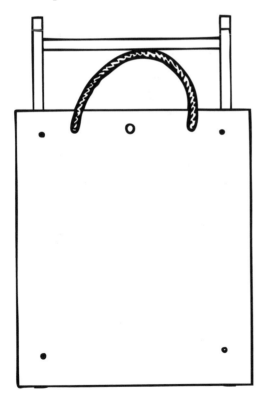

- Drill a third hole in the front center of the seat to attach a cord or rope for dragging the sled uphill.
- Find a piece of scrap wood and fix it to the floor at the front of your seat. This will enable you to brace your feet as you travel downhill.
- Sand down your masterpiece if you can delay heading for the nearest icy slope.

PLASTIC BOX SLED

Take that plastic storage box out from under your bed, remove the lid, and fling the contents on the bed. Take the box, which ideally should be around four feet (120 centimeters) long and two feet (60 centimeters) wide. It can be smaller if it is for kids. Now, drill a hole in the center of the short end. Find some cable lying around the house that you are not using, thread it through the hole, and tie a knot to secure it. Now, go find a slope.

WHEELBARROW SLED ON A BUDGET

The snow is perfect, the shops are closed, and you have no sled. Do not despair. Go to your shed and take the top of that nice wheelbarrow you never use. Then, go to the attic and take down those old skis you never threw out. Next, get some pieces of wood that are lying around the garage, along with some nails and screws, and put the wheelbarrow top on the skis. Screw your wood to the top of your skis and your wheelbarrow to the top of the wood. This should go nice and fast. It may not stop until it hits a tree.

FOR THOSE UNABLE TO BUILD

If you are challenged by even the most basic DIY activity, there are still ways for you to create your own sled. Do you have a metal trash can that has no handle on the lid? If it has a handle, can you break it off? Turn the lid upside down. Sit down and bend your knees, bracing your feet on the rim of the lid. This will move at a good pace down a slope. You will not be able to control your speed or direction in this sled, and you may turn in circles as you descend. Perhaps you should consider asking a less manually challenged friend to drill two holes in the front of the lid. Attach a rope handle. This will give you some control. If you attach two smaller rope handles, one on each side, you may even be able to steer it a little.

You can also use a large metal or plastic tray as a sled; any other hard, flat object that you can fit yourself on is also worth trying out. Laundry basket lids, unused satellite dishes, or an old car hood will all work well.

87

BUILD AN IGLOO

When faced with subzero temperatures and a snow-covered landscape, an igloo is man's ultimate shelter. A well-built igloo can keep you snug as a bug at a temperature of up to 60 degrees Fahrenheit (16 degrees Celsius), even as temperatures outside plunge to 40 degrees below zero. Two or three people can easily build an igloo large enough for themselves in an afternoon, and with some care, the structure can last until the thaw. The only tools you will need are a lot of snow, a small saw, a shovel, and a spare pair of gloves or mittens.

GETTING STARTED

Choose a site for your igloo in an area where the snow is approximately three feet (one meter) deep. Stomp vigorously over the whole area for half an hour to properly compact the snow. Let it rest for another half an hour and then use a piece of wood or a ski to trace a circle, about six feet (two meters) across, in the surface of the snow. If you are all very tall, make it a bit bigger; at its widest point, the finished igloo needs to be bigger than the largest person in your group.

Cut down into the base of the igloo to make blocks of snow. Their exact size will vary, but a good guide is about 18 by nine

by 12 inches (45 by 25 by 30 centimeters). They need to be light enough for you to lift. If the snow at the base of your igloo is less than three feet (one meter) deep, you may want to stomp out another area of ground to make an additional "snow quarry" a few feet or meters away from your intended site. Do not worry about making your blocks perfect at this stage, as they will be cut to fit during the building process.

THE BUILDING BEGINS

As you start building your igloo, bear in mind that it will be built in a spiral shape, with each ascending layer leaning in slightly more than the last to create the familiar domed profile. To help this happen naturally, begin your first row with a triangular block. Before you position each

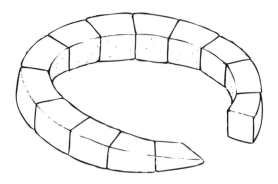

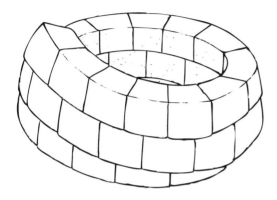

block in place, carve a slight arc out of the base and trim the edge so it can fit against the last one. Hold it at the appropriate angle against the last one, and then gently slide it down and into place. The edges of the block will compress slightly, causing the block to stick firmly in place. As you complete each layer of blocks, cutting a very slight slope into the top will help the next row of blocks lean in toward the center of the structure.

Keep building and you will see your igloo take shape. Before the wall gets too high,

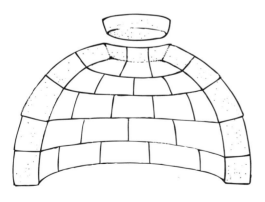

one of you will need to stand inside the igloo and help with construction from there. Keep going until your igloo is almost complete, with just a small opening at the top. At this point, those of you on the outside will need to cut a reasonably circular block for this hole. Trim the sides carefully so that it matches the tapering of the hole. Get the person on the inside to stand directly underneath the hole to help maneuver the block into place, like the lid on a Halloween jack-o'-lantern. Pack loose snow into any gaps or cracks, and your dome is now complete!

THE ENTRANCE

The eagle-eyed among you will have realized that your igloo has no door and that your gallant friend appears to be stuck forever in the igloo's icy womb. To solve this difficulty, carefully saw a small arch-shaped entry into the side of the igloo. This entrance should only be large enough to crawl through, and should face away from any prevailing wind, or your cozy snow-hole won't be so cozy after all.

Cut and stack a number of smaller blocks to create an L-shaped wall around your entrance to stop snow from blowing in and allow your friend to escape.

FINAL STAGES

The last step is to trim any protruding edges on the inside of the igloo and to smooth the sides down with gloved hands. Your gloves will get very wet—this is why you've brought a spare pair. This completely smooth surface will stop drips from forming and falling onto you.

Your new snow-home is now ready for you to move in. Lay a carpet of plastic, blankets, or camping mats and set up camp. You can use a stove to cook inside your igloo, but cut a small ventilation hole in the dome first. As you use your igloo, your body temperature will cause the snow to melt and refreeze, strengthening the structure even more. After a few days of igloo life, it will probably be strong enough to stand on.

So lie back, snuggle up, and take comfort as the arctic winds howl around your snow-sanctuary of warmth.

88
AVOID DEEP SNOW AND AVALANCHES

It is very tiring to travel over deep snow. If snow is more than one foot (30 centimeters) deep, you should consider wrapping your feet to make your footwear more waterproof. Deep snow will obscure natural hazards such as thin ice, edges of a ridge, loose rocks, unexpected hollows, or uneven ground. Deep snow on hilly terrain will involve a risk of avalanches. Proceed with caution.

TREE WELLS

If you are traveling in an area where the snow is deep, you should assume that deeper snow and hazards might be around. Tree wells occur when the area beneath the tree is sheltered from falling snow by the lower branches. The area around the trunk becomes a hole or void. If heavy snow occurs and the lower part of the tree is obscured, this hole can be more than six feet (two meters) deep. Each year, skiers die when they fall headfirst into tree wells. If you fall headfirst into a tree well while skiing, you have a 90 percent chance of remaining stuck and dying if unaided. All tree wells are signposted by a tree.

PLACES TO AVOID

Do not travel in deep, snow-filled gullies and try to avoid travel on steep, snow-covered mountains.

When you are traveling, you should watch out for avalanche tracks. You will see a large, vertical channel of missing trees with a pile of snow and debris at the end.

On high slopes, the prevailing wind will often scour the windward side of the slope and blow loose snow on the lee side. If wind scouring is evident, travel on the windward side of the slope. Loose blown snow is at high risk of slipping and causing an avalanche.

REDUCE THE RISK
OF AN AVALANCHE

Avalanches occur on slopes of more than 30 degrees and usually happen within 24 hours after heavy snowfall. If you are traveling near snowy slopes, you should remain alert to the danger of avalanches.

Do not travel the day after heavy snowfall, especially if it has not been snowing in the preceding days. Loose snow lying on compacted snow or ice is a high risk.

If you are traveling in a high-risk area, go out early in the morning, before the sun has had time to warm the ground. It is safer to travel on irregular sloping ground with trees. Trees may stabilize the snowpack, making an avalanche less likely.

Most fatalities occur in the early months of the year, but May is also a dangerous month since late snow, coupled with thawing ice, can trigger a slide.

IS THE SNOWPACK SAFE?

If the snow is compacted, it should be relatively safe and not prone to the cracking or slipping that creates avalanches. Signs of a loose snowpack are cracks on the surface of the snow and small slabs dislodging. You should also listen for hollow sounds as you walk that indicate loose snow underneath.

If you have a snow shovel, dig a small hole about four feet (120 centimeters) deep near where you suspect an avalanche may start. Then, press your shovel down vertically behind the back of the pit and pull the handle. If the layers of snow pull away easily, the snow is very unstable, and if small tugging results in some layers moving, it is still unsafe. If strenuous effort is needed to move the snow, you can proceed with caution.

DO NOT START AVALANCHES

Avalanches occur due to a variety of factors, including temperature, snowfall, wind, the angle of the slope, snowpack stability, and vegetation. If the conditions are right, it may only take the weight of one intrepid hiker to trigger a slide, which may carry the hiker, and anyone unfortunate enough to be directly below, down the mountain in a hurry. Avoid walking on or moving unstable snow in high-risk areas.

89
FIND SHELTER IN A SNOWSTORM

If you get stuck in a snowstorm, you will not be able to construct a time-consuming shelter like an igloo. You will need to stop traveling and gain shelter immediately to prevent hypothermia and to avoid getting lost or injured by traveling in poor visibility.

IN A CAR

If you get caught in a snowstorm in your car, do not abandon your vehicle. Consider opening the hood so that any passing rescue vehicles will know you are in distress. Tie a colored piece of material to the antenna of your car to attract attention. Make sure that your exhaust pipe is not blocked with snow so that you can periodically turn on the engine to heat the car. Open the window a little to allow fresh air into the car, especially if it is running, to prevent carbon monoxide poisoning. Put on all available clothes or blankets that are in your car. Move around as much as possible to keep warm, but do not leave the car.

TEMPORARY SHELTER

If you are outside and there are no buildings or vehicles around, you will need to construct something hastily. The longer you are exposed to the wind and wet, the higher the risk of hypothermia.

If you are close to trees, try to find one that has blown down. You can climb under the branches of a partially felled tree. Use nearby branches or leaves to make this shelter as windproof and waterproof as possible and light a fire at the entrance to keep warm and stay dry. Make sure you do not lie directly on the ground. Use whatever waterproof material, dry greenery, or extra clothes you have to raise you above the cold, wet ground.

If the snow is already deep, you may be able to dig under the lowest branches of a partially submerged tree. The tree branches will then provide a roof and you will be out of the wind. Again, line the ground with whatever you can find before you sit or lie down. This shelter will not allow you to light a fire and is only useful as a temporary measure.

If you happen upon an unoccupied cave, you should definitely take advantage of it and move in, lighting a fire and at least partially covering the entrance to keep warm. A whole cave may be hard to find. Densely packed bushes and boulders can be turned into a shelter by adding some branches cut from nearby trees and using waterproofs, pine branches, moss, leaves, and even your backpack as a bed. This will probably be a little cramped. Clear a space for a fire at the entrance if you can. Then curl up and wait it out.

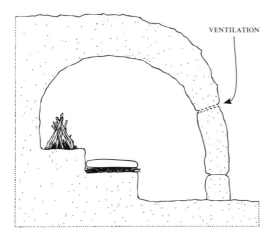

VENTILATION

DIG A SNOW CAVE

A snow cave will provide good insulation and a more comfortable solution to your sheltering needs. Build this if you are about to be caught in a snowstorm and are unable to reach a vehicle or civilization but have time to build.

A shovel or two will greatly hasten the construction of your snow cave. If you are not so fortunately equipped, use sticks or branches.

You will need to find a snowdrift about 10 feet (three meters) deep. If you cannot find one quite this big, pile up surrounding snow to this height, pack it down a little, and then commence digging. Dig down into the drift and then climb into the entrance and dig upward. Ensure that the roof remains arched so that all melting snow drains off of it. A flat roof will either melt or collapse. Continue to hollow out the drift. The walls should all be at least one foot (30 centimeters) thick for proper insulation and stability.

Now, build a platform at the back of the drift for sleeping. This should not touch the sides. Build a trench around the sides of your cave so that melting snow from the walls and ceiling drains out the door. Your bed should be off the floor, but low enough so you can sit up and not hit your head. Build a fire at the entrance. Never cover the door completely, especially if you light a fire.

90
AVOID FROSTBITE

Frostbite occurs when the soft tissues of your body are exposed to the cold and freeze. The early stages of frostbite do not usually result in permanent tissue damage.

SIGNS OF FROSTBITE

In the beginning, frostbite will affect only the surface layer of exposed or cold skin. Itching and pain are the earliest signs of frostbite, although you may notice the area feeling cold first. This leads to skin discoloration, with red, yellow, and white patches appearing, followed by numbness in the area. This mild form is sometimes known as frostnip.

If you remain in a cold environment after the onset of frostbite and do not treat it, it will get worse. The skin will freeze and become hard to the touch, although the deeper tissues underneath will remain pliable. Within one or two days after suffering from frostbite of this severity, you will experience blistering in the area.

If frostbite continues, the muscles, tendons, nerves, and blood vessels will all freeze. The area will feel numb, hard, and rubbery to the touch. Blisters that appear purple and may be filled with blood will appear on areas that have suffered this degree of frostbite.

DANGERS OF FROSTBITE

The early stages of frostbite will not usually result in any long-term damage. If any blistering has occurred, then there is a chance that the area affected may be permanently insensitive to touch, cold, and heat.

More advanced frostbite requires medical treatment as quickly as possible. Amputation of fingers and toes is not uncommon, as gangrene may set into the areas that have frozen. Even if surgery is not necessary, the area may suffer permanent loss of feeling. Long-term consequences may include cancer, increased sweating of the skin, and arthritis in the area.

AVOID FROSTBITE

Prevention is the best cure. You will be more susceptible to frostbite if you are wearing inadequate clothing, are wet, have been drinking alcohol, suffer from poor circulation or are wearing clothing or shoes that impede circulation, are diabetic, suffer from exhaustion, or are a smoker.

If you are traveling in a group, have a system in place so that each person is checked periodically by another for signs of frostbite. Check the face, hands, and any other exposed parts regularly for the early signs and treat quickly.

Do not drink alcohol in extreme cold, as it increases the risk of hypothermia and frostbite. Wear adequate clothing. Periodically place your gloved hands over your face and ears to prevent them from getting frozen. Wiggle your toes in your shoes to ensure that they are not freezing. Keep your gloves on your hands and periodically place your gloved hands next to your body. Remove wet clothing immediately.

TREAT FROSTBITE

You must get warm and treat frostbite quickly. It is extremely important that you do not allow frostbitten areas that have been warmed to freeze again. This will increase the tissue damage. If you are unable to stay warm, keep traveling until you can reach medical aid and can stay out of the cold before attempting to warm the frozen skin.

Do not treat frostbite by rubbing the area or applying snow to blisters. Light a fire or get indoors or into a shelter away from the cold and wind. Warm the face and ears with hands and warm feet by placing them on a volunteer's stomach. If frostbite is severe, do not attempt to treat it. Get out of the cold and get medical help.

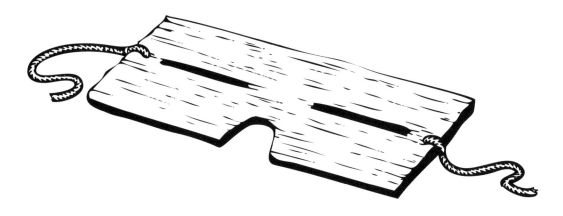

91
COPE WITH SNOW BLINDNESS

The sun reflects off the white of snow and ice and can expose your eyes to harmful ultraviolet rays. Exposure to these rays can cause permanent damage to your eyes.

PREVENTION

Wear correct sunglasses with 95 to 100 percent ultraviolet protection to protect yourself from snow blindness. Buy glasses that are designed specifically to block blue light and that wrap around your face, protecting your eyes at all angles. In addition, you may wipe soot under your eyes. This will reduce the glare to your eyes further.

It may be tempting to remove your glasses as they get fogged up while hiking, or because you wish to take photos. Whether the day is cloudy or sunny, your eyes can still be harmed and your glasses should remain in place. If you find your lenses are getting misted up and you are unable to see, you can pull your glasses slightly away from your face. This will enable cold air to clear the lenses. It will also prevent your eyes from being completely protected from the sun's glare.

If your glasses break or they are permanently fogged up and you are unable to see, you might consider making your own eye protection.

Rip off some birch bark about three inches (eight centimeters) wide and long enough to wrap around your head as far as your ears. Cut a triangular slot for your nose. Then, measure the bark against your face and make two very small slits for your eyes, the thinner the better. Use your hat to keep the glasses on. If you have no hat, then make holes in the bark and tie it to your head with shoelaces.

Duct tape may also be used to create these glasses. Remove the tape from your face very carefully once you have moved indoors.

SYMPTOMS

The symptoms of snow blindness will not show up until a few hours after your eyes have been overexposed to ultraviolet light. You will experience watery eyes that will then become bloodshot. Your eyes will feel gritty and will feel sore if you move them. You will experience a headache that worsens with continued exposure of your eyes to any light.

TREATMENT

If you wake up in the morning unable to see, or suffer from signs of snow blindness, take action. You can purchase eyedrops that will aid recovery. You should completely cover your eyes with material until all symptoms cease.

Remove contact lenses if you experience any symptoms. Use a cold compress, then put on gauze or other material to block out all light from your eyes.

Rest for 12 to 48 hours with your eyes completely covered; the longer you rest, the better. Eyedrops specifically designed to aid healing from snow blindness can also be used in conjunction with covering your eyes. Retinal hemorrhaging can occur in severe untreated cases of snow blindness and needs urgent medical attention, as it can result in permanent blindness.

92
GET RESCUED FROM SNOWY AND ICY TERRAIN

SIGNAL FOR RESCUE

As with all terrains, you should use all available methods to signal for help. If you are using fire to draw attention to yourself, try to place synthetic material, rubber, plastic, or oil on the fire. This will generate black smoke that will be visible even during the day.

STAYING SAFE WHILE AWAITING RESCUE

To prevent accidents, tie the members of your group together and anchor yourselves to the ground or to a slope while you await rescue. Pitch a tent if you have one, or use all available materials and supplies to create a makeshift shelter to protect you from the elements. Use a buddy system in a group, so that everyone has someone checking them for signs of frostbite, hypothermia, shock, or altitude sickness. One person needs to take charge of the situation to ensure that everyone stays positive and calm and that all supplies are rationed.

RESCUE A FELLOW HIKER FROM A CREVASSE

If a fellow hiker falls down an icy crevasse, do not delay in rescuing them. If necessary, lower a rope, loop it around their legs, and pull them up. It may not be possible to wait for professional help due to the high risk of death from hypothermia. The air temperature in a crevasse is significantly lower than that above ground.

GET RESCUED FROM AN AVALANCHE

If you are traveling in a high-risk area for avalanches, you should be equipped with an avalanche beacon, which you need to set to transmit at the start of your expedition. This will enable you to be found quickly by search parties.

Having shovels and ski poles will enable you to look for victims yourself. If a buried victim is not found in the first 15 to 30 minutes, there is very little chance of survival.

SURVIVE AN AVALANCHE

If you get caught in an avalanche, try to remain calm. If you have triggered the avalanche, try to jump up the slope above where the snow is slipping. This is unlikely to save you, but it is probably worth trying.

Run sideways if an avalanche starts above you. Even if you are caught in the slide, it will be moving more slowly at the edges than in the center, so you will be more likely to survive. Running or skiing downhill will not help you escape, as avalanches can travel up to 180 mph (300 kph).

Once the snow begins to move below you, try to ditch all of your belongings, which will simply weigh you down. Try to ski or to remain upright for as long as possible. When you fall, adopt a swimming stroke. This should keep your head above the snow longer.

Once the snow begins to slow down, you will be buried. How deeply you are buried will depend on how long you remained floating on the surface, how much of the avalanche was behind you, and how big the slide was.

Before the snow comes to a complete stop, cup your hands around your mouth to create an air pocket.

Digging yourself out is a good idea, if you think you are relatively close to the surface. If you are too far from the surface, you may simply exhaust yourself and deplete your limited air supply. Once the snow stops, move your arms and legs to create some space around you. If the snow was wet, it will freeze almost instantly. You may be disoriented and confused. Allow yourself to drool a little and pay attention to the direction gravity pulls the drool. Now dig in the opposite direction, toward air.

If you hear rescuers, you should call out and then wait. Remember, you only have about 30 minutes of air. Try to remain cheerful. You will probably pass out from lack of oxygen and the onset of hypothermia, regardless of what other injuries you have sustained, well before you become aware you are suffocating.

BOOK EIGHT

CLIMATE AND TERRAINS OF THE WORLD

93
TEMPERATE CLIMATE

A temperate climate occurs in parts of the world between the latitudes of 40 and 60 or 70 degrees north or south. It is neither as hot as a tropical climate, nor as cold as a polar climate. It has four distinct seasons with variation of both temperature and rainfall. It can be cold and snowy in winter and hot and relatively dry in summer. To experience this climate type, travel to countries such as Spain, Italy, France, and other coastal countries in Western Europe. Canada, much of the eastern United States, and areas of Russia and China also have this climate type.

TEMPERATURE AND RAINFALL
The average temperature of the coldest month is between 27 and 65 degrees Fahrenheit (minus three and 18 degrees Celsius). Within temperate climates, there is a wide variation in the temperature range and rainfall within the seasons depending on where you are. In forest areas, rainfall can reach levels of 20 inches (500 millimeters) per year and average annual temperatures are about 50°F (10°C).

ISSUES
In the Northern Hemisphere, more people live in areas with this climate than elsewhere.

High population density is not the only issue, though. Large-scale intensive farming is also prevalent in this climate because it is easy to grow many crops and raise livestock here. For both of these reasons, you are less likely in temperate regions than in many other places on the globe to find yourself in true wilderness.

PLANTS AND ANIMALS
This climate, even in its wild, natural state, has fewer and less varied types of plant, insect, and animal life than in more tropical regions. It also has fewer hazards to the adventurer. Coniferous, deciduous, and mixed forests are abundant in these regions, where they have not been felled to give way to farming. While some snakes, leeches, ticks, and mosquitos are present and you may happen upon a bear, a cougar, or an unfriendly squirrel, you are less likely to die from your interaction with life outside than elsewhere in the world.

In temperate forests, many animals naturally hibernate and many birds migrate to escape the winter. Deciduous trees lose their leaves in the winter, and food for wildlife or intrepid foragers becomes scarcer. You may come across squirrels, deer, black bears, raccoons, weasels, mice, rats, porcupines, and wild turkeys.

Plants like moss, ferns, and mushrooms thrive and trees like beech, birch, and oak are common. A variety of pine trees can also be found in mixed forests.

SURVIVAL IN THIS CLIMATE

This is perhaps the easiest climate to survive in as a human, as long as you are not traveling unprepared in winter. The changes of season will provide the biggest challenge to survival.

During the late spring through the middle of autumn, you will be able to hunt, forage, and find water and shelter with ease. As the autumn progresses, the wildlife will either migrate or hibernate. To survive, you will need to store and prepare your food and shelter in advance or move south for the winter.

94
MEDITERRANEAN CLIMATE

You'll find a climate of the Mediterranean type in the countries of the Mediterranean basin, which are Spain, Portugal, North Africa, Italy, Greece, and Turkey. It is also present in parts of southwest South Africa, West and South Australia, coastal Chile, and California. All areas with this climate are between 32 and 41 degrees of latitude either north or south of the equator and are adjacent to large bodies of water.

A Mediterranean climate can be described as one in which olive trees can be successfully grown.

TEMPERATURE AND RAINFALL

In this climate, you'll experience almost rainless summers that can vary from warm to hot. The average temperature in the warmest month is above 70 degrees Fahrenheit (22 degrees Celsius). In most regions, the average high summer temperature is 86°F (30°C). The average annual temperature is above 50°F (10°C); in many areas, the average low winter temperature is as high as 55°F (13°C). The winters are mild and almost all of the rain occurs during the winter months. Most areas receive about 20 inches (500 millimeters) of rainfall annually. There are really only two seasons, winter and summer.

ISSUES

While most people find this climate type very desirable, there are some drawbacks. Coastal areas are more prone to frequent fog. Many areas can experience a complete lack of rain for four to six months of the year. While plants can adapt to these conditions, these droughts make farming and water management in cities difficult. Many areas are prone to summer fires due to the lack of rainfall.

PLANTS AND ANIMALS

Vegetation in this climate must be able to survive long, dry months. Many plants are dormant during the summer months. Evergreen trees like pine and cypress thrive here, as do some deciduous trees like oak and sycamore. These areas are famous for grapes, olives, figs, and citrus fruits. Bay trees are also native here, as are lavender.

There are few large grazing areas. Areas with this climate are naturally home to sheep, goats, and horses. The wildlife varies depending on the precise region. You can find rabbits, jackals, foxes and lynx, skunks, and pumas. Insects that you may come across include the honeybee, the ladybug, and the praying mantis. You may also find lizards here, such as the alligator lizard.

SURVIVAL IN THIS CLIMATE

This climate, due to the arid nature of the summer months, makes survival difficult. You are unlikely to suffer from hypothermia, but you may have difficulty finding water in isolated areas or foraging for food. Much of the world with this climate type is highly populated, with cities such as Perth, Los Angeles, and Rome. Other areas are highly cultivated. This makes a situation where the need for long-term survival is unlikely, as you are probably always within a day's trek of human habitation.

95
ALPINE CLIMATE

At higher altitudes all over the world it is possible to find an alpine climate. The temperatures are cool at their warmest and the air pressure is low. These two factors combine to produce a unique environment that provides a challenge to all forms of life. Plants, animals, and explorers must adapt to survive. You may experience this climate by traveling to any mountain range, such as the Rocky Mountains in North America, the Andes in South America, the Alps in Europe, Mount Kilimanjaro in Africa, Mount Fuji in Japan, and the Himalayas in Tibet. This climate exists at latitudes higher than 10,000 feet (3,000 meters) above sea level.

TEMPERATURE AND RAINFALL

An alpine climate can be found at various latitudes because altitude is the deciding factor in determining this climate type. At a certain elevation, known as the tree line, trees fail to grow and give way to grass, moss, and other adapted alpine plant life. At this altitude, the annual average temperature can be as low as 34 degrees Fahrenheit (one degree Celsius). The highest altitude at which a forest will grow well has an average annual temperature of between 42°F (6°C) and 54°F (12°C). Precipitation averages about nine inches (230 millimeters) annually. At these altitudes, the weather can change rapidly. Warmer summer weather of 50°F (10°C) can change to freezing winter temperatures in the space of a day.

PLANTS AND ANIMALS

Plants have had to adapt to this climate. Many shrubs grow low to the ground to escape the wind, and flowering shrubs hibernate during the winter. Many only flower once every two years for a couple of weeks. Tall trees or plants are not present, as they would quickly blow over or freeze. The soil is not of good quality, as plants do not decompose quickly enough in the cold climate and soil is blown away in the high winds. Plants that survive here must be able to live in dry, sandy soil.

Snakes and other reptiles do not live in this climate. Insects are found here; some are native, while others migrate over high mountains. You may come across beetles and grasshoppers. The animals here have adapted to survive the lower oxygen levels, cold, and high levels of ultraviolet radiation. They tend to have larger lungs and have short legs, tails, and ears to reduce heat loss. Animals that you may see in these regions include the llama and the alpaca, the chinchilla, the mountain goat, the snow leopard, and the yak.

SURVIVAL IN THIS CLIMATE

There are many barriers to survival at high altitude and in extreme cold. People who live permanently in these regions of the world, such as the Indians of the Andes and the Sherpa people of the Himalayas, have adapted over hundreds of years to life here. They commonly have more blood cells and hemoglobin to enable their bodies to deal with the high altitude.

To survive, you need to acclimate yourself to higher altitudes over time, and be prepared by traveling with specialized gear, including oxygen. Proper cold weather clothes, tents, and extra food and fuel are necessary. Foraging for food is very difficult.

Even with these precautions, you need to be alert to signs of altitude sickness, hypothermia, and frostbite.

Sudden changes to the weather, blizzards, getting lost, falling down the mountain, or getting caught in an avalanche are all possible survival challenges you may face.

96
TROPICAL CLIMATE

Tropical climates occur in the latitudes between five and 35 degrees on either side of the equator. They have high temperatures year-round, and usually have two seasons in the year, a dry season and a wet season.

TEMPERATURE AND RAINFALL
The average temperature in the tropical regions is 65 degrees Fahrenheit (18 degrees Celsius) year-round. Except in the rain forest, the rainfall varies hugely depending on the time of year. There is no dry season in a tropical rain forest. The total amount of rainfall varies slightly from month to month, but temperatures are high, constantly averaging 80°F (27°C), with humidity higher than 77 percent. Total annual rainfall can be more than 100 inches (2,500 millimeters). Tropical rain forests are found in a narrow band of five to 10 degrees from the equator, but can be as far as 25 degrees north of the equator. Specific areas include the Amazon basin, the Congo basin, and the East Indies in a stretch from Sumatra to New Guinea. Tropical rain forests now cover only six percent of the world's surface because of deforestation and the growing human populations in these places.

PLANTS AND ANIMALS
Everything grows in abundance in the rain forest, including bacteria. It is home to a huge variety of plant, animal, and insect life. It is estimated that half of all of the world's animal and plant species live here. Nearly three-quarters of all the plants here are trees, and they provide more than 40 percent of the world's oxygen.

The animals of the rain forest vary depending on which forest you are in, and even where you are in each forest.

All rain forests contain various species of monkeys; you can also find bats, exotic birds such as the toucan, an array of snakes and other reptiles, unusual animals such as the sloth, large animals such as the elephant and rhinoceros, and predators such as the tiger.

SURVIVAL IN THIS CLIMATE
Fresh water is always available in this terrain due to the daily rainfall. Food is also abundant, although the high temperatures and humidity make food go bad quickly. The rain forest is also home to many poisonous spiders, insects, and plant life. Any bite, cut, or graze is also more likely to become infected.

MONSOON CLIMATE

This type of tropical climate exists in South and Central America. It is also present in southwestern India and southwestern Africa. The climate is dictated by the changing direction of the monsoon winds. The air moves off the sea during the hotter sunny season and changes to move off the land in the cooler months of the year. Temperatures remain high throughout the year with very little variation, while the rainfall varies hugely. Large amounts of rain fall during the months of high sun and there is usually a short drought in the less sunny months. The seasons are described as rainy and dry.

PLANTS AND ANIMALS

This climate is ideal for flora and fauna and boasts the richest areas of biodiversity in the world. Many animals have become highly adapted to the climate to survive. The Indian elephant would starve if the monsoon did not produce new grass for it to eat every year. The giant gharial crocodile lays its eggs to coincide with the monsoon. The rains prompt many plants to grow and trees to produce fruit. Many species of birds and monkeys rely on these annual fruits.

SURVIVAL IN THIS CLIMATE

Traveling in the monsoon period is usually not recommended. Roads and villages are routinely swept away in sudden downpours. This makes camping and hiking difficult.

97
TUNDRA AND POLAR CLIMATE

TUNDRA CLIMATE

The tundra is found at latitudes of 55 degrees and 70 degrees north in the area surrounding the North Pole. It is cold, stark, and treeless and covers about 20 percent of the world's surface. To see it, you need to travel to the coastal areas of the Arctic of North America, the coast of Greenland, northern Scandinavia, or northern Siberia in Russia. During the summer you may experience daylight for up to 24 hours a day, while during the winter there are weeks where the sun barely rises at all.

TEMPERATURE AND RAINFALL

There is no true summer here. Winter is very long and is broken by a period of slightly milder weather. In the tundra, the coast prevents the temperatures from being as severe as in a polar climate. There are only about eight inches (200 millimeters) of precipitation a year in the form of snow here, and you can expect temperatures to fall as low as minus eight degrees Fahrenheit (22 degrees Celsius) and as high as a chilly 43°F (6°C). In the Scandinavian tundra, the temperature may reach 54°F (12°C). It is also windy. It is not a place to book a summer holiday.

PLANTS AND ANIMALS

There are no trees here because the ground is permanently frozen three feet (one meter) below the surface, so roots cannot spread. There are very few plant species here, and these consist mostly of moss, lichens, and grasses. The tundra does boast 400 types of flowers, although these are only visible for about 60 days a year.

Animals do live here, although only warm-blooded ones. Caribou, also known as reindeer, live here. You can also find foxes, wolves, bears, rodents, polar bears, rabbits, and hares. There are fewer than 50 varieties of mammals, which is a very small number.

Insects can survive here. There are mosquitoes, deer flies, and other biting insects, especially in the summer months. The snowy owl lives here, and migrating ducks and geese may also be seen.

SURVIVAL IN THIS CLIMATE

It may be possible to live here during the summer, if you don't like it to be dark at bedtime, as there will be food to hunt and fish. During the winter, it would be advisable to migrate south.

POLAR CLIMATE

The polar climate is found in the Arctic and Antarctic. Inland Greenland, northern Scandinavia, northern Iceland, areas of northern Canada, and Siberia also experience this climate. It is characterized as an ice cap climate. No plants grow here. There is no summer or any month with an average temperature above 32°F (0°C).

PLANTS AND ANIMALS

A gap in the ice may allow you to fish. In the Antarctic, you may happen upon a penguin. If you are close to the coast in the Arctic, you may see a polar bear. If this happens, you may need to run away.

SURVIVAL IN THIS CLIMATE

Explorers have ventured to these areas. Specialized gear is essential. Survival is not guaranteed, despite all precautions, preparations, and equipment.

98
SAVANNAH AND DESERT CLIMATE

SAVANNAH CLIMATE

Savannah is a type of tropical terrain where there is a large difference between the amounts of rainfall depending on the time of year. The average temperature is about 60 degrees Fahrenheit (16 degrees Celsius), as it is cooler in the wet season. The dry season typically experiences less than two inches (50 millimeters) of rainfall.

Areas where this climate occurs include the Northern Territory of Australia, Florida, the Serengeti of Africa, and areas of India, Brazil, Indonesia, Mexico, Haiti, and Tanzania.

PLANTS AND ANIMALS

The African savannah is home to giraffes, zebras, hyenas, baboons, lions, and many other identifiable species. In Australia, the savannah is home to emus, dingoes, kangaroos, koalas, wallabies, possums, and saltwater crocodiles. Reptiles of all types thrive in savannahs.

Most of the rivers in a savannah climate dry up during the dry season, and many animals migrate to look for food.

Plants in all savannahs are usually limited to long grasses with some scattered trees. The prolonged dry season limits tree and shrub growth. In Australia, the acacia and eucalyptus tree thrive.

SURVIVAL IN THIS CLIMATE

The savannah is home to many predators. The prolonged dry season, coupled with high temperatures, makes this a difficult place to survive. Sudden heavy rain in the wet season can lead to flooding, which poses additional risks to safety. There is little in the way of shelter from the elements, and very little plant life to forage. Other better-adapted species are likely to take the best hunting opportunities. Even if you are successful in hunting, you may find it difficult to keep your kill.

DESERT CLIMATE

There is more than one type of desert. All deserts are arid; that is, they experience so little rainfall that they are unable to support plant life except scanty scrublike vegetation. There are both hot and cold deserts. Hot deserts are found roughly 15 degrees to 28 degrees north and south of the equator. Famous deserts of the world include the Sahara in Africa, the Sonora in North America, the Kalahari in Southern Africa, and the Great Australian Desert.

The Great Basin desert of North America is an example of a cold desert. It stretches from the Rocky Mountains to include the

Mojave and Sonora deserts and includes the Sierra Nevada mountain range. The high altitude and winds off of the Pacific Ocean create the dry desert conditions. These desert areas occur between 4,000 feet (1,200 meters) and 6,500 feet (2,000 meters) above sea level.

TEMPERATURE AND RAINFALL

Hot deserts have annual rainfall of less than six inches (150 millimeters) a year. Cold deserts may have as much as 10 inches (250 millimeters) of rain and snowfall a year. The Northern Territory of Australia experiences more rainfall than this, but the evaporation rate is so high it is still classified as a desert. Hot desert climates have an annual average temperature of about 65°F (18°C) and the highest annual temperatures may reach 120°F (49°C). Cold deserts experience mild summers and very cold winters. They may have areas permanently covered in ice.

PLANTS AND ANIMALS

Both hot and cold deserts have few plants, and most animals and insects burrow underground to escape the extreme weather. In hot deserts, many animals stay dormant during the day, coming out only in the early morning or at night. Lizards live here, such as the armadillo lizard of Africa, banded Gila monster of North America, or thorny devil of Australia. Birds like the cactus owl or the cactus wren may be spotted in

Mexico and the southwestern United States in semiarid desert areas. Warm-blooded animals like the bobcat, coyote, or desert rat can be found in North American deserts. In the Sahara, there are dung beetles, horned vipers, monitor lizards, and the death stalker scorpion. You may be more pleased to find a camel or an ostrich. In the Kalahari, you can see lions, jackals, meerkats, giraffes, and even antelope. The larger number of animals here is due to the much greater diversity of trees and other plant life.

Plants in the desert are specially adapted to the hot, arid climate. Many plants have evolved to flower and produce fruit within hours of rainfall and ripen and die within three days. Other plants grow roots up to 80 feet (25 meters) long to take advantage of underground water. Cacti survive by storing water inside and having a tough, waxy exterior that protects them from harsh sunlight.

SURVIVAL IN THIS CLIMATE

Survival in the desert is usually dependent on your ability to get out of the hot, arid area as soon as possible and into a more habitable region. If you are well supplied with a suitable shelter from the elements and have huge quantities of water and food, you will not die. As you will be unable to replace your food and water to adequate levels, death may occur eventually if you insist on staying.

BOOK NINE

YOUR EXPEDITION

99
HOW TO RECORD A JOURNAL OF TRAVEL

First, you will need a notebook and a pen. This may be a little old school, but it is not dependent on batteries or a continual supply of electricity. If you leave on your journey equipped with a stylish notepad and one or two nice pens, you will at least have started with the right intentions. Make it sturdy, so that it does not fall apart and you do not lose precious pages. A nice spiral-bound notebook may be best.

START RIGHT AWAY

One of the biggest mistakes people make in creating a journal of this type is waiting to start until something notable happens. Start the first page with your thoughts the night before you set out. Commit to curling up in your sleeping bag and jotting down your day's events and your thoughts every night. This may lead to some dull entries such as, "It rained and the fire took two hours to light," but it will get you writing.

MAKE IT PERSONAL

You are not writing the next best-selling novel, but you should consider that if you are lost in the wilderness and the notebook is found next to your skeletal remains 10 years from now, it will have a certain grisly appeal. If you make it home in one piece and fail to get mauled by a bear, stared down by an alligator, or chased by a squirrel, then the journal may be just for your own enjoyment. The more personal you make your journal, the more you will enjoy reading it yourself in 10 years.

Consider adding a note such as, "Mike is driving me mad and I am considering putting a spider in his shoe," to your previous entry about the fire, for instance.

DETAILS

It is interesting to note the details of the countries you are traveling in and how they differ from day to day. Writing down the number of the bus or the number of people on the plane may be stretching this a little. What you ate for lunch is not that interesting unless it was roasted rat or deep fried locust. Details to include are the date of each entry and where you are, including the name of the place you stayed. If you are camping, this may be vague.

ARTISTIC DETAILS

To make it more interesting, consider a scrapbooking approach. Have you got an interesting ticket to add or can you sketch the centipede that just bit you?

Adding color by using different pens, or even pressing flowers or leaves you find to add in, will make the notebook more interesting. Even bad cartoon sketches will add humor. If you plan on recreating Mike's expression when he found the spider in his shoe, you may want to keep your journal private.

KEEP MOTIVATED

It may seem that you have been writing about rain for a week, but do not despair. It is amazing how amusing misery can seem once a few years have passed and your hypothermia is a distant memory.

Details that you record may prevent you from returning to an area on later expeditions only to realize that you forgot you hated it there the first time.

On a more positive note, you can avoid eating that plant that looked like a dandelion, find that great campsite again, or be reminded how much you prefer camping alone by quickly referencing your journal before your next expedition.

100
FOR FURTHER READING

An important step to becoming a true adventurer is to be as well informed as possible. Many of your fellow adventurers by sea, land, and air have written accounts of their experiences. They can inspire you to follow in their footsteps and prepare you for what you may find. Adventuring in the world of nature has also inspired many novels and stories. Here are a few of the most popular fictional and real-life adventures to begin with.

FICTION

Treasure Island
By Robert Louis Stevenson

The Adventures of Huckleberry Finn
By Mark Twain

Robinson Crusoe
By Daniel Defoe

Around the World in Eighty Days
By Jules Verne

Twenty Thousand Leagues under the Sea
By Jules Verne

In Search of the Castaways
By Jules Verne

Call of the Wild
By Jack London

White Fang
By Jack London

The Swiss Family Robinson
By Johann D. Wyss

Moby Dick
By Herman Melville

In Our Time
By Ernest Hemingway

A River Runs through It
By Norman Maclean

NONFICTION
The Age of Exploration

The Travels of Marco Polo
By Marco Polo
Marco Polo is said to have inspired Christopher Columbus himself to be an explorer. It may be a good idea to plan some vacation time before reading this, just in case you are similarly affected.

The Four Voyages: Being His Own Log-Book, Letters and Dispatches with Connecting Narratives
By Christopher Columbus
In this work, you get to read Columbus's own log book, letters, and dispatches to get

a glimpse into the mind of one of history's great explorers.

Over the Edge of the World: Magellan's Terrifying Circumnavigation of the Globe
By Laurence Bergreen
This book is inspiration for the sailor in all of us. It recounts the life of Ferdinand Magellan, who sadly died before his expedition of 1519 completed the circumnavigation of the globe. He is now famous enough to have a penguin, a galaxy, and lunar craters named after him.

The Journals of Lewis and Clark
By Meriwether Lewis and William Clark
On their brave expedition from the Missouri River to the Pacific Ocean in 1804, Lewis and Clark mapped waterways and recorded the flora, fauna, and natives they found on their travels.

The Sea

Adrift: Seventy-six Days Lost at Sea
By Steven Callahan
What happens when you are cast adrift on a life raft, in the Atlantic Ocean, with few supplies, and beset by sharks? Read this book to find out.

The Perfect Storm: A True Story of Men Against the Sea
By Sebastian Junger

In real life, the sea often defeats even the most experienced fishermen.

Life in the Woods

Walden
By Henry David Thoreau
In the 1840s, the American writer Henry David Thoreau lived in a cabin in the woods near Concord, Massachusetts. This book recounts his thoughts and experiences during his stay.

A Walk in the Woods
By Bill Bryson
The Appalachian Trail extends 2,200 miles (3,500 kilometers) through the mountains of the eastern United States. This book is an introduction to the places, wildlife, and people to be found hiking along the trail.

The Desert

Arabian Sands
By Wilfred Thesiger
Thesiger was the first Westerner to cross "The Empty Quarter," which is one of the largest expanses of desert on earth. He did so on two occasions between 1946 and 1949, mapping the terrain as he traveled.

Skeletons on the Zahara: A True Story of Survival
By Dean King
The story of 12 American sailors who were

shipwrecked off the coast of Africa in 1815 and then survived a journey through the Sahara Desert, this book is sure to give you a thirst.

The Sky

Wind, Sand and Stars
By Antoine de Saint-Exupéry
The author flew over the Sahara and the Andes delivering mail in the 1920s and 1930s. This poetic, philosophic work may inspire you to get those flying lessons. This book is translated from the original French.

Alive
By Piers Paul Read
In 1972, a group's plane crashed in the Andes and they were forced to eat their own dead to survive. Would you like some tomato sauce with that?

The Mountains

High Adventure: The True Story of the First Ascent of Everest
By Edmund Hillary
The first man ever recorded to summit Mount Everest in 1953 gives his own thrilling account in this book. It is a must-read for any aspiring mountaineers or armchair hill walkers.

Into Thin Air: A Personal Account of the Mt. Everest Disaster
By Jon Krakauer

In 1996, a rogue storm killed eight climbers and stranded many more on the slopes of Mount Everest. This climber gives a chilling personal account of the tragedy.

High Exposure: An Enduring Passion for Everest and Unforgiving Places
By David Breashears
A look at one man's passion for Mount Everest, this book is sure to inspire you to seek higher altitude.

Between a Rock and a Hard Place
By Aron Ralston
This man actually hacked off his own arm with a pocketknife. To find out why, you need to read this book.

The Ice and Snow

South: The Endurance Expedition
By Ernest Shackleton
Read in Shackleton's own words just how bad it gets when your ship gets stuck in ice in the Antarctic, forcing you to get out and walk.

Endurance: Shackleton's Incredible Voyage
By Alfred Lansing
This well-told story of how the famous expedition in the Antarctic turned into a harrowing fight for survival is an exhilarating read to be enjoyed in the warmth of your own home.

The Worst Journey in the World
By Apsley Cherry-Garrard
One of the survivors of the Antarctic expedition led by Robert F. Scott tells his story about a journey that he did not exactly enjoy.

The Wilderness

The Darkest Jungle: The True Story of the Darien Expedition and America's Ill-Fated Race to Connect the Seas
By Todd Balf
In 1845, a group of explorers tried to find a way through the jungle of Panama to connect the Pacific and Atlantic Oceans. It is only about 100 miles (160 kilometers). What could go wrong?

Through the Brazilian Wilderness
By Theodore Roosevelt
What happens when you do not get reelected as president of the United States? You almost get yourself killed by getting involved in an expedition on the Amazon River, of course.

Jungle: A Harrowing True Story of Survival
By Yossi Ghinsberg
This is what actually can happen to you if you head off backpacking in the jungle and get lost.

Into the Wild
By Jon Krakauer
This true story is about a man who decided to abandon the cares of the modern world and head to Alaska to be alone in the wilderness.

The Final Frontier

A Man on the Moon: The Voyages of the Apollo Astronauts
By Andrew Chaikin
Read this because everyone dreams of undertaking this adventure, but so few can fit into a spaceship.

INDEX

INDEX